A Rewritten Story

SURVIVAL, STRIP CLUBS AND SALVATION

A Rewritten Story
By Dr. Tyra Hodge

Visit Author page TyraHodge.com
Copyright @ 2023 by Dr. Tyra Hodge
ISBN – 979-8-9875538-8-6 (paperback)
ISBN – 979-8-9875538-1-7 (hardcover)
ISBN – 979-8-9875538-9-3 (eBook)
ISBN – 978-0-578-36856-6 (KDP)
ISBN: 979-8-387-64553-2 (KDP Hardcover)

All rights reserved. No part of this publication may be reproduced, distributed, or transmitted in any form or by any means, including photocopying, recording, or other electronic or mechanical methods, without the prior written permission of the publisher, except in the case of brief quotations embodied in critical reviews and other non-commercial uses permitted by copyright law. For permission requests, write to the publisher at the address below.

In accordance with the U.S. Copyright Act of 1976, the scanning, uploading, and electronic sharing of any part of this book without the permission of the publisher is unlawful piracy and theft of the author's intellectual property. Thank you for your support of the author's rights.

The names of real people have been changed to protect their identities. I would like to thank the real-life people portrayed in this book no matter what their role was in my story. I recognize that their memories or interpretations of the events described in this book may different than my own.

Permission: For information on getting permission for reprints and excerpts, contact:
Hodge Publishing
Conroe, Texas
Info@Hodgepublishing.com
832-292-5864

A Rewritten Story

SURVIVAL, STRIP CLUBS AND SALVATION

DR. TYRA HODGE

Acknowledgments

I must say thank you to my Heavenly Father for being with me and guiding me every step of the way. Thanks to my family the one thing God gave me to have to fight for. To my students that have reached adulthood God still has a plan for your life. It is a good one and some of you are living it.

Contents

Acknowledgments	v
1. Present Day-2022	1
2. Arlington, Virginia - 1974	5
3. Daddy Issues	9
4. "F" School	15
5. The Man at The Park	21
6. Houston, Texas 1981-1990	27
7. Junior Year	35
8. Senior Year	39
9. Houston, Texas 1995	45
10. Trafficked	57
11. Traumatized	65
12. Missing All the Turns	73
13. Living is Hard When You are Dead	77
14. The Baby Blues	83
15. Wichita Falls	89
16. The Call	97
17. Back to School, Back to Life	105
18. The Turning Point	113
19. The Gruesome Twosome	117
20. Job Hunt vs. Husband Hunt	123
21. A Marriage Made in Hell	127

22. God's Purpose: What He Really Wanted from Me	135
23. Good Things Come to Those Who Wait	143
24. Best Job Ever	153
25. I Saw the Sign	159
26. The Birth of Some New Ideas	165
27. To New Beginnings	171
28. The Second-Best Year Ever	175
29. Life Anew	177
30. Fallout	183
31. Family Ties	187
32. Something Unexpected	193
33. Nothing is without Challenges	203
34. The Voice	209
35. Doc. Hodge	215
36. Conclusion - Facing Demons	225
Epilogue	
Lessons on Family	237
Lessons on trusting God and His plans	238
Lessons on God, Faith, and Humanity	239
Lessons on Mistakes	241
Lessons on failure and success	243
Lessons on Love and Abuse	245
Lessons on Determination	246
Phoenix	247
Lesson on Contentment	248

1

Present Day—2022

A dark figure peered up through the second-story window of the building from the outside parking lot. Its eyes were locked on its soon-to-be young victims. The teenagers could sense its chill and hunger right from where they stood. They would not escape. Not now, not ever.

"She doesn't scare me," Rolando locked eyes with the figure two stories down and refused to be moved. "Besides, she won't catch us." His confidence was distressing for the others with him.

"She said she would catch us next time. We should have listened." The female began to shake her hands in nervousness.

"Dude, quit staring out the window."

"I'm not moving. I'm not running from her." The beautiful female gently tugged on Rolando's open cuff. But Rolando ignored her.

"Dude, get out of the window. She is going to see us!" Her voice was laced with fear as she increased the pressure on Rolando's cuff.

"She's already seen us." The advice which fell on deaf ears.

The two boys and a petrified female tried to run down the stairs, hoping that they could get away. The trio made their way down the stairs to find the dark figure about to enter the glass door at the bottom of the steps. In a desperate attempt to escape, the triad ran back up the stairs and through the door. Their pursuer picked up the pace but never once came to a run. The dark figure then whispered something into the top right side of her chest where her radio sat.

Two of the caramel-colored teens began to hyperventilate in panic as Rolando rejoiced at the thrill of the escape and a solution to their dilemma.

"Quick into the bathroom!" he exclaimed.

As the teens turned the corner of the second floor, they suddenly realized there was another figure approaching from another hall. They rounded another corner, got to the restroom door, and came to an abrupt stop. It was like hitting a brick wall. The bathroom door was locked. They would not get away, after all. They huddled together in fear, waiting for the worst to occur. There was no other way around it. Two people approached from opposite sides, getting closer so slowly that time seemed to join in the procession. Hands held up to their side, and like an answer to their waiting, they were caught.

"Rolando, Rolando, Rolando," the dark figure spoke. "How come, how come every time I am in the hallway, you in the hallway? It is blatantly obvious why *I'm* in the hallway, because my job won't let me have it any other way."

"Ms., you know what? You are always blocking. And you know what else? You like Covid, Covid-19, because you won't just go away."

The female gave Rolando a glare that held a lot of unspoken meaning, the most prominent being a plea to keep his mouth shut. But that wasn't going to halt his free-flow of self-expression. I had to say, though, in all these years, I have been called so many things, and I have always been able to rationally detach myself from the feeling that came with it. But being called Covid? That actually stung!

I glanced over to my partner, Van Way. He caught my eye, and we both knew we had to keep a straight face because if not, we would have immediately burst into laughter.

"I'll tell you what," Van Way started in. "We'll let you know if we'll go away in a few minutes. Follow me." Turning to me, he asked, "Doc Hodge, you got the back?"

"Always, brotha." I replied enthusiastically, pleased about the great capture we just collected.

I noticed that the female had dropped her backpack and tried to leave it by the water fountain. When the trio began to follow Van Way, I quickly snatched up the backpack and took my place behind the students.

Rolando could not help himself, not like he had ever been able to. "Why do we have to follow this bald-headed nigga, when we just need a tardy pass?"

"My dear sweet Rolando, two minutes past the bell is tardy. Maybe. But twenty minutes past the bell is far more than tardy. It is called skipping."

I heard Van Way mutter "most definitely" from the beginning of the line, affirming what I maintained. We made it to Van Way's office and told the triplets to have a seat. The female's eyes lit up with fear when she suddenly realized I had the backpack that she had dropped earlier. Her expression only gave me more confidence that Rolando would finally be headed to DAEP today.

I turned my head to my radio and spoke with the confidence I had groomed throughout the years. "I'm going to need a female to help me search, and we will most likely also need an officer to transport."

"What you mean a search?" That squeak came from the female, fear amassing in her pretty eyes. "We were just skipping."

"I thought y'all were just tardy?" Good o'le Van Way. I chuckled for a second.

"We weren't causing any harm," Rolando finally muttered in a low voice, seeing as there was no other way around it. "A search is totally unnecessary."

"Why don't you let us be the judge of that?" Excitement coursed through my bones, and there was a light spring in my steps as I moved away from the radio to face the three.

"There's no getting out of this now, is there?" I smiled into their petrified faces. "Easy there. I promise to go easy on you. I don't bite, and Van Way certainly doesn't either."

"This wouldn't have happened if you had listened to me, Rolando." The female whispered in a shaky voice, hands over her auburn hair.

"It would still have, you know?" I was having a good time with this. "I never go back on my promises, and I wasn't going to start with y'all. Remember what I told you the last time when I saw you out of place?"

The trio sighed all at once as if orchestrated by a choir. It was going to be a long day for these youngsters in jail. It was also going to be a long day of paperwork for this principal.

Arlington, Virginia – 1974

It happened in the dead of the night. I remember my typical 3-year-old brain thinking about the cartoon I had seen earlier that day, wondering if the superpowers portrayed would suddenly manifest in me by the time, I woke up the next morning. I couldn't tell at what point I dozed off, but the feeling of someone suddenly grabbing me from my crib jerked me back to consciousness.

"Mommy?" I couldn't tell in the pitch dark, but I knew it definitely didn't feel like her hands. "Mom is that you?"

The hands lifted me out of the white baby crib that was positioned across the stove, by the back door of the small kitchen downstairs. The townhouse had only a few bedrooms, and mom said there wasn't any more space upstairs for my crib. If there had been, maybe that night wouldn't have occurred.

Even if I didn't understand a thing about the act of kidnapping at that age, I knew something was wrong the moment the owner of the hands didn't reply. There were no windows around my crib, and thus I couldn't make out the person's face. Maybe I should have screamed, but nothing came out of my mouth, even as the hands carried me out of the kitchen and into the driveway.

I think it was fear that had my mouth clamped shut. *What were they doing? Why were they taking me out? Did Mommy send them?* It took me so long to understand what they were up to.

Out in the driveway, I could see their faces clearly. It was a black woman and a white man with very long hair. They seemed to be closer than expected as the man led the woman into the car, holding her waist. The woman held on to me tightly even as I squirmed in her arms. The car was already running, and we drove out, seemingly far away from the townhouse.

I asked, "Where is my mommy?" My face scrunched up in frustration.

The couple looked at each other for a second, and then the white man spoke: "Tyra," He started slowly. "This *is* your mother." They looked at each other again, not convinced they were doing the right thing.

Surprised that the man with the long hair even knew my name, I paused and stared in confusion.

"Where is my mommy?" I asked again. "Take me back to my mom!" I whined loudly, deciding to play the role of a needy and demanding child. Many years later, I realized that I must have sounded like a brat. I could feel my eyes tearing up.

"Tyra, this is your mom." The man didn't get frustrated with me when I started to cry. His voice was almost soothing.

"Tell her," the man said to the black woman.

The woman turned to look at me in the back seat. "Tyra, my name is Anna Mae." She explained slowly, looking me in the eyes affectionately. "And I'm your mother. The lady you were living with is your aunt, my sister. She has been caring for you because I had to be somewhere else. I'm home now, and I came to get you. So, stop crying."

It took a lot of adaptation and acceptance, but it wasn't as hard as I feared it would be that night. It wasn't even comparable to what I had to face later on. But at that moment, new realities were birthed for me.

During that period, I learned that my mother had gotten pregnant with me in her senior year of high school. I imagined how lonely she must have been, trying to go through it all without the assistance of the person who was responsible. She was without direction, going through those tough times like they were going to be her final passage on Earth. Maybe I wouldn't have been born, had that continued to happen for a lengthy amount of time. Perhaps, it would have been too much for her to handle.

But she didn't have to go through it all alone. After some guidance from her sister, she finished high school and was forcibly made to go into the Navy. My mother explained how she was trying to do the best thing for me. She said she thought about me a lot and wondered if I was fine. Her sister, the person I had called mommy for three years of my existence, had assured her I would be completely taken care of.

Later, when I was five, I visited my aunt's house again. But I dreaded it. I remember shaking in fright as I approached the townhouse I had once called my home. I could not face being teased and humiliated by the boys again, having to lock myself up in the bathroom for fear of being found. They all stared at me that day as I walked in, my eyes too low to avoid looking back at any of them. I went into the kitchen, the same one that had my crib behind the door. It brought back memories I had left untapped, and for the hundredth time that year, I was relieved I hadn't screamed that night my mother came to get me. If I had, I might have still been trapped there.

I did not want to have to explain, but my mother needed me to show her exactly what the boys had done that made me not want to return. All I could manage to say was, "The boys were trying to make me have a baby."

She was confused, and for a split second, thought I was just cooking something up. "What do you mean, baby?" She asked, wrinkling her forehead as if in deep thought.

"They were trying to make me have a baby," I repeated slowly, not knowing what else to say.

I could not explain it correctly, probably because I did not want to have to narrate what had been happening to me. And besides, I was just five. Was it any surprise that a 5-year-old child would have trouble explaining that she had been in inappropriate sexual situations? I was humiliated and embarrassed. But being sent back at years old I knew it wasn't right. I wish

I could have taken back my disclosure, because I was just sent back to my aunt's house. There were times I hated the other children. At just five years old, I knew and felt hate. I wanted them to care for me like friends were supposed to, not to make me feel nasty and gross. As a result, I hated them for failing to be my protectors and for becoming my predators.

Daddy Issues

Daddy issues are one phenomenon that is all over the talk shows and regularly appears in pop culture. Lawyers use this as an excuse to try to get criminals off. But the problem with daddy issues is that they can sometimes give people a warped image of our one true father: God.

My own father's situation left me with quite a few Daddy Issues, and they, in turn, affected my relationship with others. I have a biological father who chose not to make himself available to me as I grew up. This hurt a lot, especially as a teenager. But, when I was younger, I had a stepdad who was proud of me. He loved to take me everywhere with him. He would take me with him to get his hair cut, to the park, to hang out with friends, and even to strip clubs.

At the strip clubs, all the women seemed to know him, giving him weird smiles and winks each time he got close. Back then, I didn't think it was strange that he took me there to hang out. It was called a Go-Go Bar. If my mother had known that this was where he spent his time and that he had taken her 5-year-old daughter with him, she would most certainly have been angry. I realized that he used me as an excuse to get out of the house. He didn't want my mom to interrogate him about where he was going, so he took me to help with his cover story. He took me everywhere. Whatever his reasoning, the fact that he was not ashamed of me, despite him being white, made me proud. Strip clubs aren't the best place for a father-daughter quality time, but I was happy to be getting his attention, even if it involved making up stories about where we had been when we got back home.

Although some things were normal and positive about my stepfather, his other side was not nearly as fun. Almost every weekend, he would get drunk and become angry about something, so much that it became a dreaded routine. Sometimes he became so angry that he ripped things apart in our Virginia apartment. When he acted like that, my mother and I had little choice but to leave, choosing our safety and mental health at that moment. But days later, he would always come back, pleading like a man who had lost his only means of obtaining happiness in life. My mother always ended up forgiving him, and we would find ourselves right at the point we had left.

One night he came home drunk and angry, and my mother wanted to leave as usual. Furious, my stepfather wrapped a hand around my neck and lifted me off my feet, threatening that if she left, he would slit my throat. He had a pocketknife at the tender part of my throat, and I could feel the sharp blade pricking my skin. The sharp blade was bad enough, but I was also losing consciousness from the way he had me suspended in the air, his hand crushing my throat. Hanging there on the wall, I tried to squeeze out, "Daddy, please." I was so scared that he would cut me. I wasn't really afraid of dying – just of getting stabbed. I imagined the bloody mess that would have been everywhere, most especially on the couch mummy had earlier made me clean.

"Leon, don't!" my mom screamed. "Please put her down!"

"You don't have the right to order me around," he yelled drunkenly, still holding on tight to me. "It is meant to be the other way around. You are my mine, and you do not have the liberty to just waltz in and out like you own the place."

"Leon!" My mother looked so scared.

"It is simple. If you walk out this door, your daughter's life is over. And you know I don't make empty threats." I wondered what he meant by that.

Weeping, my mother fell to her knees in complete surrender. Tears were also streaming down my face. "I won't leave. I won't leave!" my mother cried. "Just put her down."

After he finally let me down, I crumpled to the floor, light-headed, bruised, and gasping for air. After that day, my stepdad continued to drink and smoke his marijuana like nothing had happened. He only seemed to get wasted on Fridays, probably because it was his payday. He would always come home late, daring my mother to get upset. On the occasions that she took the bait, he would hit a wall, break a door, smash a chair anything destructive. This was always his response to my mom's confrontations. He wasn't a cruel man by nature, though. The alcohol just changed him, turning him either into an abusive person or a playful one. I never knew which one we would get each weekend. It was like waiting to be surprised.

There was another time I had gotten in trouble for something I can't seem to remember now. I was six years old at the time, naive and clueless. Whatever it was, my crying irritated my stepdad. He yelled at me to shut up, but I couldn't. I was too upset. He began to pace beside me, whispering, "shut up, shut up." My inability to stop only agitated him further. His pacing grew faster as he grabbed the roots of his hair. In a sequenced swoop, he picked me up and threw me to the floor. He took the sharp tip of his boot and slammed it into my side. We both screamed out, but for different reasons.

I screamed out in pain. He did it out of the shock of the pain he had just inflicted. My dad fell to his knees beside me and pleaded for forgiveness.

"I'm sorry, I'm so sorry." I knew he was genuinely repentant, but it didn't soothe the pain I felt in my ribcage for weeks, nor aid the bend in my walking pattern during that period. I never told my mom just because he begged me not to. His apology had seemed so sincere as he cradled and rocked me in his arms.

"Forgive me." He pleaded again after giving him no response. "I didn't mean to do that."

"Okay," It didn't matter if he had meant to do it or not. I was still going to forgive him.

But now I wonder why I never told my mom about this episode. Maybe it was because, at the time, I so wanted my stepdad to love me. This was like our thing, a secret we could share and build a relationship upon.

One night, I stayed up with my dad all night while he was drinking. We pretended that we were taking the Lord's Supper. I broke up the little pieces of white bread and placed everything onto my little China set plates, which I laid on the coffee table. In place of wine, my dad provided the beer. I was enjoying his company, and my sip of beer, and how he hummed softly under his breath. We had pulled all-nighters together before, and I did not mind his drinking. It was always so much fun when it was just the two of us.

Suddenly, my dad fell back into his favorite reclining chair. At first, I thought he was just fooling around, but my opinion changed a few seconds later when he just lay on the chair with his eyes rolled back. The can of beer he had been holding onto was spilling onto the floor, making this sickening sound that made the whole scene appear scarier. I took the almost empty beer can out of his hand and laid it on the table, my shaking hands making it a difficult task.

There were no sounds coming from my dad, not even the whisper of an indrawn breath. It was as if all trace of life had escaped the room. I was sure if a pin had dropped, I would have been able to hear it. Taking a deep breath, I tried to reassure myself that everything was fine when deep down, I knew something was wrong.

"Daddy," I called, shaking him gently. "Can you hear me? Wake up, wake up." There was no response, and I could only see the whites in his eyes and an almost ghostly look of shock. When I could not wake him, I went to get my mother.

"Mom, wake up!"

"Tyra, go back to bed," my mother groaned, waving her hand in the air as if shooing a fly.

"Mommy, Daddy won't wake up. He fell back in his chair and won't wake up. His eyes are open."

It was an unwritten rule that I never woke my parents when they had retired to bed, especially on weekends. I stood there for a moment until my mother finally realized that my persistence was out of character. She sat up and stared at me.

"What did you say?" The grogginess was still in her eyes.

"Dad suddenly fell on his chair and wouldn't answer me." My voice carried so much fear in it. My mother immediately jumped out of bed, hurrying to the next room.

"Leon, Leon!" She started crying, shaking him over and over again. "Baby, please, don't do this." Her voice became unsteady. As her fears began to unravel, I could only go back into the closest corner and squat. Mummy tried again, but he would not wake. She called the hospital after her series of trials, but by the time the ambulance arrived, my dad was already dead. I was shocked to see that the time on the clock had not changed. Had all the clocks in the house stopped, or had time stood still?

Although my stepdad wasn't perfect, I still loved him so much. His death was very difficult for me.

After he died, I always imagined that he was not really gone, that he was somewhere lurking and waiting for the right time to reappear. I hoped that it was just a government conspiracy and that he would show back up in our lives one day. But he was dead, and alongside the little attention, he had given me. I loved my stepfather, and I believe he also loved me in his own way.

My stepdad's funeral was held at the Arlington National Cemetery; however, his body was eventually buried in Indiana in a separate funeral arranged by his family. The stopped clocks in the house remained unfixed for days after my dad's death. On the second night after his death, I could have sworn I saw his shadow lingering next to my bedroom closet, staring. I could not explain such things, but that would not be the only time when such mysteries have visited me. Strangely, I wondered what he wanted.

After my stepdad died, my mom suddenly began to go to church, finding succor and strength in the ambiance of the holy place. More so, mom chose to stay single, deciding that there would be no more abusive men in her life. Still, after seeing what my mother had gone through, I had unconsciously internalized the pattern that abusive relationships tended to have: the cycles of disappointment, pain, and forgiveness.

I realized over the years that the various studies in journals that conclude how parents are such an important influence in their children's lives are no joke. They are preaching the truth. Having a good set of parents to look up to for morals and guidance is one of the biggest blessings anyone could ever wish for. I sometimes think of my mother and what she must have gone through just to put up with an abusive partner.

Not having a father figure in my life would sometimes make me think of Pearl from *The Scarlet Letter*. Although I mainly identified with Hester, at times, I also identified with her illegitimate daughter Pearl. Neither Pearl nor I knew of an earthly father, only a heavenly one.

"F" School

It is not novel that school sucked for me as a child, so much that the memories all got mucked up in my head. I remember this: two white girls fighting over me on the playground, their hair flying all over the place as they pulled me by my arms. They held on tight, their anger and distaste for each other apparent on their faces. It reminded me of a video game I played, away from my mother's prying eyes, where we controlled the tennis rackets as the white ball bounced back and forth.

"My black friend," one of the girls said, breathing heavily like she had run a marathon. She had one hand on me and the other on her waist and would have passed for a black woman who was scolding her child.

"No," the other girl disagreed. "This is my black friend!" She tugged on without a care in the world, and I was stuck helplessly in their middle, watching as they argued over me like I was a piece of property. This is the most attention I ever got on the playground' nothing even remotely close.

| 15

With my eyes closed, I endured it all, hoping it would pass as quickly as it had started.

Kindergarten is the year that kicked off my extended career in education. Like most kids, I had a pretty soft-spoken teacher who would only make a fuss about the things that directly affected her. I don't remember her name, but I can recall that she never actually spoke to me, not even when we had to turn our assignments directly to her. One of my tug-of-war buddies was working next to me, only assuming that title when she was mad with her friend and needed to take it out on my poor arms. Outside of that, she never talked to me, either. It was like I was almost invisible, only brought out of the fog when the need arose. I would have been comfortable with that had it been the same with the rest of my classmates. But it seemed like she had a personal issue with me, and I remember asking myself a few times if my mother had done something wrong to her that she thought to take it out on her child. It was a whole lot of confusion, heightened by the occurrence of a gloomy Tuesday morning.

That day, the teacher with beautiful blonde hair and blue eyes was walking by, and suddenly, my classmate asked a question, making her halt. "Is my picture pretty?" she asked, looking up at the teacher expectantly.

"Yes!" the teacher responded, nodding like her words weren't enough. "That's a beautiful picture." I saw my teacher smile and continue to walk by, suddenly feeling the need to have that acknowledging smile directed at me too. It had never happened since I started schooling there, and I had no idea why my childish mind suddenly thought it would be different on that day.

Wanting some of that adoration as well, I finished my picture really quick, making sure I got all of my strokes and color blends correct, then waited for her to make her way back to my table, with the click of her heels signaling her approach.

"Is my picture pretty?" I asked in the same tone as my classmate, expecting a similar response. My picture was held up in excitement, and I did not have to wait long for her perusal.

"No, it's ugly," she said upfront, not bothering to hide her displeasure at the young student she was meant to be protecting. That same pretty little teacher's face had scrunched up, and she almost hissed at me. I saw the disgust etched all over her features, but I had no idea what I had done. My painting was better than that of the girl she had given a favorable response to a few minutes ago, so it definitely wasn't that.

My embarrassment and shock were enough to keep me from doing any more school for the next nine years without feeling a tad bit terrible about it. It felt like my actions were justified, and I was only a victim that didn't want to experience another embarrassing situation again. I went to school like a robot each day, unable to keep my eyes away from the clock. Once, I wished Aladin wasn't a fictional character and that he would come with his lamp, asking me to make three wishes. I wanted my first to be the vanishing of everything that had to do with academics, but I had no idea that it was only a small part of my problems.

But I was held back both in first and second grade, made to suffer the consequences of the decision fueled by my experience that day. My teachers often told my mother I only came to school to eat and didn't give a thought to anything termed academic. That was funny to me because, at the time, I hated my browsuaggert sandwich, apple, moon, or oatmeal pie - the only meals that seemed to accompany me to school each day. I hated it all and was always hungry, never getting to satisfy any of my cravings. I did always envy the hot lunches served at school, but I knew I wouldn't be getting any of those. So, in the end, school sucked, as well as lunch.

Apart from the issues at school that tormented the state of my mental health and that of my stomach, there were also other things I had to go through. After my dad died, weird things would happen, like someone throwing a brick through our basement window with the words "Nigger" written on it. This kind of shook up my family a bit, even though it was hard to admit since we were considered too young for those kinds of discussions. My mother, after the attacks, thought it was time for a change and packed us up, moving us to Arizona along with one of her sisters and her kids. It was a piece of excellent news for me, as I got to leave my old school and not see the disgust on my teacher's face each time I walked down the school's hallway. I wouldn't also be stuck eating the food I hated so much.

My mom was excited about having a new start, except when the date for her wedding anniversary came. She would stay in bed for most of the day, not even coming out to wish us a good day in school. It was the normal procedure for years after my father's death, and I began to get used to it. It ceased to bother me as much as it used to because it became the norm. I, for one, was going to take advantage of my new start as well. It was a new school, so I had the opportunity to decide who I wanted to be there, maybe pick up some friends and even better lunch.

The school year started in Arizona, and things were not that exciting at all, but rather far from what I had envisioned. The desks in the classroom were shaped in a horseshoe arrangement, and we had to be sitting in an awkward U. The classroom was surrounded by windows on both sides, perfect for all the pretty wild adventures that would be hidden in my brain. No one particularly liked me or talked to me. I was alone in my space, and it gave me the opportunity to venture into another one of my mind's caught-up realities. It became my nine-month routine, thinking, unthinking, and rethinking so much that I preferred being in my imagination more than talking to actual people.

On a sunny afternoon, as I walked home from school, one of the girls came up to me, riding her bike. My first instinct was to be excited to see someone from school out in the open, without the usual constraints and restrictions that came with a classroom setting. I thought this would be a new opportunity to finally have a friend, and with a smile, I anticipated my move. The little blonde girl from my class circled me with her bike, and I only felt obligated to say something.

"Hi," I said with excitement, willing to break the ice.

The girl then stopped circling me and in a firm roll of the bike, aimed directly at me. She rode it with precision and intentionality, but even at that point, I wouldn't still have thought it purposeful. I thought it had to have been an accident until she began to say, 'Nigger! You're a nigger,' all the while hitting me with her bike. So much for wanting to start a friendship.

I proceeded to continue my walk home with tears streaming down my face after she had finally left me alone. I began to hyperventilate as I walked faster to my home, scared that someone else who shared the same opinion as herself would head for me too. I made it home without another attack, then went into the bathroom and stared at the mirror, hurt and broken. The thing was, I wasn't scared of the little girl, and if the situation were to have been different, we might have made good friends. My feelings were not hurt due to her actions; instead, I was angry that I didn't hurt her back in the same measure she did to me. Everything inside of me wished I had lashed back at her, throwing her off her bike and probably using it to hit her too. It was easier to protect myself than it was to be on the receiving side of her anger. But I had stood there, doing absolutely nothing.

The next day at school, the little blonde girl did not even acknowledge that I existed, walking past like I was a part of the fading decoration on the wall. It was like the day before had never even happened, like she hadn't even met me at all. Her mother happened to be there that day in school as a speaker for one of the organized conferences. I considered it odd that a woman with a vicious daughter was addressing a host of parents, who only wanted the best for their kids, but who wanted the opinion of someone as young and neglected as I was.

I decided that I would let her mother know what she did, even if it meant getting the attention I would have rather stayed away from at that rate. I walked over to her mother, sitting patiently beside her as she addressed the parents, saying something about an all-accepting community for children of different races and statuses. As I listened, I was slightly relieved as I thought she would listen and understand since, after all, she was a lover of an all-accepting academic community. I lightly touched her shirt to gain her attention, but she quickly brushed my hand away, brushing her shirt as if I had stained it. I thought she had probably not noticed me since she was so absorbed in communicating her idea and decided to try again. She turned abruptly, looking at me with disdain and disgust. I knew then, even then, these people hated me just because of the color of my skin, and no matter of theory and speeches was going to change the state of their mind, built over the years as a result of their notion of us; the same ingrained into them by their parents and grandparents.

But the thing was that I didn't understand it. I could not understand it. What was so different about their skin? Why was I made to suffer for a skin color I didn't even ask to be given?

The Man at The Park

That day, I sat by the window in the morning, wondering why the weather refused to smile at me. It seemed like the cosmos was against my plan of sneaking out that morning, as the clouds all gathered in a spot with gloomy faces like the earth was mourning the loss of a loved one. During breakfast, it took a lot to pull me away from the window, but I could still see the clouds from where I sat opposite the kitchen windows, silently pleading that a miracle would occur. Maybe the cosmos was trying to communicate something to me, but what would a nine-year-old girl in pigtails understand about reading signs in the weather?

I had slept off on the cushion my grandmother liked sleeping in when the rays of the sun touched my face. In my unconsciousness, I heard my mother yell for my cousin to wake me up. I thought about getting up myself, then remembered that there was a high chance I wouldn't be able to leave the house if they knew I was awake. So, I let my cousin, Rayray, try to wake me up. He tapped my shoulders and shook my arms when he saw I wasn't responding. After a few attempts, I pretended to yawn and whine about being disturbed, then went into the room like I was going back to bed. I didn't get up until I was sure the whole house was busy with something and had totally forgotten about me. But that didn't take so long, as it was not novel that I hated being disturbed while asleep. I sneaked out through the window in my room, satisfied when my feet made a soundless thud on the grass. I had been practicing that move for a while now, and I felt proud that my efforts had paid off. But as I strolled through my street, consciously checking behind me to see if anyone followed, I had this gnawing feeling to return to the house and embark on the short trip some other time. But my stubborn self wasn't going to listen, especially when I was already halfway there. And the worse that could happen was my mother finding out, right?

The park wasn't so far from my house, so I was there in a few minutes, standing on my toes to locate the exact spot I had planned to sit. That was when I saw him. I remember him staring at me with a smooth young-looking face to be sitting on such a contrasting face. He would steal glances at intervals, then return to watching the kids in the swing, smiling now and then like he was enjoying the show. Now, I wonder what must have been going through his mind at those times. Did he feel like he was wasting his time with the view? Or was the wait worth it? I turned back a few times to look at him for reasons different from his. Perhaps it was his eyes; they seemed so bright and piercing, like they could see into one's soul from a glance. The hair on my skin stood upright as I shivered at the thought, then I abruptly shook my head, scolding myself for believing everything I saw in the movies. He was just an innocent man enjoying the view in the park, just like every other regular person around. So rather than fret about him, I continued my search, grinning when I finally saw them.

I was interested in seeing nothing other than the young women who stretched their bodies at awkward angles at the far end of the park. My little legs carried me there, and I sat on the long bench opposite the group, watching with rapt attention as their bodies moved them as far as they would go. I was fascinated by the human body's flexibility and how much it seemed to endure. The ladies did not in any way seem to be in pain at all, so just like every youngster with a million and one dreams, I decided to be a yogist, concluding that it would be so much fun coming into the park daily to stretch for a living.

Twenty minutes into watching them, I noticed that the young man had forgotten all about his previous fascination with the toddlers on the swing, coming around the park to join me on my bench. I thought nothing of it, as I was engrossed in the art that was playing before me. At least, not until the man turned to stare at me, angling his head. Now that he was right in front of me, I could see that his face was only a feature he probably liked on himself, as he looked nothing older than his mid-twenties. He probably had just finished college and was trying to get a job.

"I think I know you," he said, squinting, like reducing the amount of light entering his eyes was going to, in any way, disclose my identity to him. "Do you come here often?"

I shook my head shyly, as I wasn't really into talking to strangers after a series of lectures from my mother.

"Then where do I know you from?" he continued, closing his eyes to think about it.

Noting that it was rude to say nothing, I whispered, "I saw you while I was coming in, and I thought I had seen you somewhere before too." It was a fat ass lie that I don't even know why I told, but it had just felt right and natural at that moment. Not saying it might have made me feel like an idiot in front of him.

"Oh, really?" he said, still not opening his eyes.

I turned back to the yoga show in front of me, diving right back like I hadn't been distracted a few seconds ago. I hoped the man wouldn't remember where we had met and would just get up and leave. He snapped his fingers after another few seconds, and I was forced to look back at him. What did he want now?

"I'm a teacher in your school," he said, opening his eyes. "You probably might not recognize me because I don't teach your grades. But you can ask those in the fourth grades. I'm Mr. Cain."

I nodded as he spoke, understanding why his eyes had seemed so striking when I first saw him. It was probably something he used to coax students into doing what he wanted them to without necessarily using any form of punishment.

"What's your name?" his voice came out more subtle than before, and I smiled up at him. Taking that feature away didn't make him as scary as he looked the first time.

"Tyra," I answered with a shy smile.

"You enjoy yoga?"

I felt proud of myself for knowing something that a teacher knew too. My teachers had always told me that I did not learn as fast as my peers, and it felt good to actually know something.

"Yes," I reply. "It's beautiful."

Cain nodded, returning his gaze to the ladies. From the corner of my eyes, I saw him pull out a notebook at intervals, glancing at the book. It was during one of those moments that I saw the time and jumped down on my feet abruptly. There was a high chance my mother had noticed I was gone, and there was no way I could avoid the scolding that would follow. I was about to run as fast as my tiny feet could carry me when Cain got up.

"Are you leaving now? You're yet to see the most amazing part of yoga, where they think about self-love and how much they invest that love in others."

I wasn't about to tell my teacher that I had snuck out of the house and that there was a high chance I was going to get a good beating at home. So instead, I made up an excuse.

"I have to go study up in preparation for school," I said, knowing that was what teachers loved to hear.

Cain smiled at me, patting my head in approval. "You are such a good student."

I shifted on my feet hurriedly as he spoke, praying that he would be done with it on time so I could dash back home.

"Let me give you a ride home," Cain said, watching my feet. "What do you say?"

It was true that my mother had warned me about accepting rides from strangers, but would you call someone who taught in my school a stranger? And I had to get home on time, so it was the best option I had at that moment. I made a mental note to tell him to drop me off at the turn leading to my street, so my mother wouldn't freak out watching me alight from a strange car.

We both walked side-by-side to his car, parked just outside the park. It was tan color, but that was how far from my knowledge of cars went. I sat in the back seat, as Cain had a ton of bags in the front and mentioned that there was no way he would move everything into the booth on time since I was so particular about getting home on time. In all honesty, I couldn't care less about where I sat, as long as I got home in good time.

We talked about school and my friends during the short ride, and he seemed interested in all I had to say. Cain asked questions like what I thought a friend meant and if my best friend could call me that too. I was genuinely pleased about his interest in me, giddy about the thought of showing off to my friends that I was a friend to one of the teachers in the elementary school. That was what he called me - his friend.

We were almost getting to the turn, so I told him I would be alighting there. Cain looked at me for a second, then turned back to the road without saying anything. I assumed he had heard me and would do as I asked until we went right past the junction.

"You passed my street already," I said from where I sat, scooting to the edge of the seat. "Do you want to get something on the next street?"

Cain, again, said nothing. His only response was the increase in speed and the silent click of the lock button of the car. I had no idea why he did that when I was supposed to be down already.

"Mr. Cain!" I tried again, already getting perplexed about his sudden silence. "You passed my street already."

Cain looked back at me, then nodded, admitting that he knew.

"Why aren't you dropping me off?" I asked, pulling on the handle inside. I could feel my hands shaking even as they tried unsuccessfully to pry the doors open. "I want to go home."

I knew I sounded like a 5-year-old crying for a stick of candy, but it didn't matter at that point. I thought about a lot of things as the man I called Cain drove on, like what my mother and aunt would do if I didn't come home that night. I remembered my mom's warnings about accepting a ride from strangers again, and my palms suddenly grew moist.

This wasn't good.

As I held on to the car door, hitting the window with my frail hands, I sighted Rayray my cousin close by, walking out of a supermarket with a white bag, presumably filled with groceries. I waved at him hastily, and he waved back with a confused look on his face. Cain suddenly noticed the exchange and cursed loudly, making me jump in my seat. Rayray kept on waving at the car, and Cain had no choice but to stop since another person had already seen him. As the car slowly came to a halt and the doors clicked unlock, he sighed loudly, hitting his head lightly on the steering.

I rushed out of the car in a frenzy, not stopping until I was right back at the park. I ran home but Rayray had run faster. Ray had disclosed that I had taken a ride from a stranger. My mom and aunt were waiting for me when I got home. The women took turns tearing my behind up when I got home.

My behind hurts from thinking about the hits from the belt as they landed, but still, I wonder how bad my life would have been if my cousin would not have seen me in that car with Cain. How traumatized would my life had been? Would I had even had a life to live?

6

Houston, Texas 1981-1990

My family's caravan left Arizona just as we had gone into it. Although we had only been there for a year, with little or nothing to show for it, particularly in the expression of my person, I was glad to leave. Perhaps my happiness was because I never felt like I fit in there with all the racist peers that never failed to make one feel like trash, the kidnappers who didn't care about the financial state of the families of their victims, as well as every other similar activity that went on like it was some regular show. As we left, I thought that Texas might be a new start for my family. Maybe, I would even try a little more complicated in school, giving it a little extra effort that I had never felt like putting in before.

But these thoughts were spurred up from somewhere that stored information I had probably heard about Texas; that would have been the only reason I had been so motivated. I noted that there was something different about Texas from all the other states I had visited at one point in my life. There was the mention of the KKK in Pasadena, Texas, but surprisingly, I didn't see it. However, I saw more people who looked like me and a host of others with distinct features I had never seen before; they were called 'Hispanics.' The Hispanics were a beautiful race of people with a beautiful language I hoped to learn one day. I was particularly intrigued by their physical appearances, with wider eyes and faced quite different from every other group of culture-bound individuals. It got me thinking about the biological components that made them different, and I had no idea how I aimed to find that out, given my disinterest in everything that had to do with academia. Along the line, I laughed at my feeble attempts to understand the genetic composition of homo sapiens and how it affected individuality. It always landed me right at the point I started, and soon enough, I gave up all thoughts pertaining to it.

Living in Texas was better for the most part as there wasn't that apprehension of getting ridiculed by people who ought to be friends for reasons I had no control over. I could also step out of my house without feeling the dread of something terrible happening to me. But still, I struggled in school like always, barely crawling successfully out of classes and grading. The difference here in my school in Texas was that the other students talked to me, as well as the teachers who occasionally thought I deserved attention despite my academic standing, without giving me weird looks. My struggle was still with my ability to focus, as I continually zoned out of classes, even in subjects I claimed were my favorites. Sometimes, I found myself creating a new planet in my head, and dumping all sorts of folks in it, thus playing the god factor. Then a teacher yelling out my name would bring me back to the present, and that only happened if the teacher noticed I wasn't there anymore. Subsequently, I was placed in all the basic classes with the other students who either struggled to learn like myself or were with behavioral problems that made the regular classrooms unfit for their adequate and productive learning. Despite my mother's numerous attempts to get me to reflect on what it meant to me, I was complacent with these students. But all I saw was the school's attempt to create the perfect environment for me to learn without feeling the pressure from the brilliant ones who wasted no time in flexing and showing their prowess amongst their peers. Because I had no interest in putting in more effort, it felt okay being around the kids who showed me no pressure nor desire to be removed from the basic classes.

It was amazing that by middle school, I found something that shifted my thought process into something more exciting and interesting - sports. Particularly interested in volleyball and basketball. It gave me something to work for and on, so much that it felt I was soaring in it but at the expense of my academics. I would go all out to ensure I made the team for every game we had, never missing out on training and stretch-outs. Everyone could see my efforts from me where the sport was concerned, but I still struggled with learning and the motivation to do schoolwork, hence my being stuck with the basic classes. In seventh grade, it finally stuck in my head when I always had to sit out the second half of volleyball and basketball due to my grades, as the rule was that you had to reach a certain grade minimum for a student to be allowed to play both halves of a game. It was strictly a 'no pass, no play system, and there was no way I could find my way around that. Coach Hale would always walk up and down the line of the female players to select who she could put in next at the games, and as expected, it was never me due to my horribly looking grades. I remember always wishing they would change the rules, even if it was just one time, so that I could play. But it never happened, and I had to sit there, watching as my mates ran around the court, swinging bats with smiles etched on their faces. It was a period of suffering for me, as what I wanted so badly was always taken from me as a result of something I wasn't even interested in, something I never got the hang of, no matter the energy I put into it. I knew I was good at sports because there were stares coming from my peers each time we trained. My coaches never ceased to praise my talent that had grown in such a short amount of time while still chipping in a word of advice as regards my academics. But it was so hard to get it across that I wanted to be a sportsperson without the interference of academics. But who was I kidding? There was no way I was going to have one without the other.

My mom never had the chance to come to my games much, and I understood because of how hard she worked to fend for myself and my siblings. But the one time she did, Coach Hale made a point of telling my mom that I could get a basketball scholarship one day if I could just keep my grades up. I couldn't tell what she thought about that from merely staring at her in the middle of my school's basketball court. But my mother made it a point of duty to remind me of my coach's statement from that day forward, hoping that it stuck somewhere deep in me and that it would lead to a sudden change and development of interest in algebra and quadratic equations. Sometimes, I wished I didn't have to put so much struggle too, and I could just magically pick up my book and understand everything written in it. My Cs and Ds staring at me from my report card weren't helping issues. So, by the end of the term, I had successfully managed to make a name in the school's sports team but still had never played a full game as a result of my poor results. This amounted to the fact that Scouters and recruiters never saw me as I always happened to be stuck on the bench, watching the whole action go on from that point, without the ability to put up a protest. I finally found something I wanted to do - something I could do for a lifetime, but like strong gates built with extra resistance, my academics stood there like a huge roadblock. But all I had to do was to stop seeing it as one, no matter how hard that was.

Eighth grade came around, and I began to notice some things about my friends in class, alongside those that played on the basketball and volleyball teams with me. It happened slowly that it might have gone by without my observation if I hadn't zoned out as usual in one of the classes I never enjoyed, and that was saying something. I noticed that as I developed and evolved in sports, I started to pick up some popularity amongst the folks in our school and the neighboring schools that came around for competitions. It started with the regular hellos and goodbyes from the kids at my school, then transcended to kids I didn't even know but must have noticed me at some point during a game or training. As a result, my friends began to change without my conscious efforts. Although my friends in the basic classes stayed the same, always hoping to make that 70 percent mark just to pass and move on to the other class, friends in sports, however, never had to worry about grades. Most of them were in honors classes, as they understood the need to maintain that grade if they remotely had the desire to continue excelling in sports. Some of them were genuinely interested in academics, even without the extra perks it brought where sports were concerned. I envied them as they found it easy to balance both sides as they were parts they were interested in equally, unlike me, who was stuck at a point, unable to move forward. One time,

I picked up my book to study, determined to make that subject and prove to myself that I could do it. When the report card was out, there was a pretty B sitting beside the particular subject, and I was ecstatic. But that was where it ended, with my inability to continue. But how could I when it didn't even involve a ball and a court?

One day I was in the cafeteria lounging about, as usual, praying to God that the break wouldn't end so I would not have to return to the classroom to learn about some literature scholar. While munching on the burger I had managed to get from the vendor with the money I had won at an in-house sports challenge, I zoned out again, thinking about my surroundings and the impact they could have on my person. It was during this period that I suddenly wanted to know about another change that was about to happen at school. I had been hearing about it all week in the hallways and at the back of the classrooms, and it made me worried about how it would affect the way we did sports at our middle school. So, I gathered up all my courage, which still sported legs that shook like a jellyfish and hands that never stayed still, going up to my principal, Mr. Bacarro, to ask if the change would affect me. When I got to Mr. Bacarro's office, I asked my question, stuttering all the way through. By the time I was done, I had doubted my principal would take me seriously enough to answer the questions of a stuttering young girl with consecutive failure in academics and with nothing else other than basketball and volleyball at hand. But instead, and much to my surprise, Mr. Bacarro put his hand on my shoulder and said, "this won't affect you because you're a good kid. Keep up with that, and you can be certain of a smooth and uneventful ride in this school."

I stood there with my mouth and eyes wide open. Surprised because no one had ever called me a good kid before, not even my mother at home, who never ceased to remind me of how terribly I was doing academically. No one ever called me good. No one ever called me at all. Was I a good kid after all? I thought about it as I made my way back to the classroom, totally abandoning my burger. Although my principal had called me a good kid, it wasn't an unknown fact that my grades sure didn't show it. In fact, I was subjected to learning with kids who had difficulty assimilating things and those labeled with behavioral disorders. Yet, my principal called me a good kid. I wanted to desperately hold on to that and find a new drive from it. I thought that was what I needed to prove to myself that I could accomplish something other than sports while keeping my whole life balanced. I wanted to be in the honors class alongside most of the other students on the school's basketball and volleyball team. I knew if I achieved that, I would earn a greater level of respect from them, and my mother could finally stop reminding me of how I was on the verge of throwing out a possible basketball scholarship due to my laziness. At the time, I didn't think education was worth my time, but I was considering giving it a shot because that was what good kids did. And that was who I was. Or at least, my principal thought I was.

For the few weeks that followed, it felt like Mr. Bacarro's eyes were always on me, even when my rational self knew he was nowhere around. I didn't know if there was a psychological explanation for it. Still, each day as I strolled into the school's premises with my backpack full of books, I knew I had no intention of studying, I remembered my principal's statement, and I suddenly felt like it was a subtle way of telling me that I had to make it work out; that I could make it work out. I was given a new charge to play sports excellently and, at the same time, keep my academics afloat. I often remembered the sincerity in his eyes, like he wanted me to understand what he was trying to say. And I did.

After that, I put in my best efforts, finally understanding the perks education brought to every aspect of life. I tried to study each day as often as I could and sometimes stayed awake the whole night, trying to get some equation stuck in my head. I employed the concentration techniques we used during games and found out it was just as effective where academics were concerned. Subsequently, I stopped zoning out during classes and could endure a 1-hour lecture without feeling the need to rush out of the classroom. My teachers started noticing when my hands always went up in class when questions were asked, seeing as nobody even made any attempt in the basic courses. Then our first test commenced, and this time, I wrote it with a bit more confidence than the previous ones. But even at that, I dreaded when the results came out and closed my eyes tightly as our teacher handed them in. She stopped at my table, touching me lightly on my shoulders. So, I opened my eyes then, not believing that she was actually smiling at me. In that new development, I opened my sheets, my eyes bright as they ran through the scores. At the end of the card, it was stated in bold, 'A's, B's and one C.

I did it! I could finally play A team basketball and volleyball games rather than being subjected to the bench for a whole half. All this happened because of a simple comment. I went home that day and asked my mother to write me a note to get out of the basic classes. Without any hesitation she did.

Junior Year

The summer before junior year, I went to a place called Country Camp. It was the most amazing experience. I found God. The camp was the most countrified place I had ever been. The music, other young people praising the Lord. This filled me with so much hope and life. I vowed that summer, that I would forever serve the Lord.

I kept developing in my skills with sports. I was becoming a stronger volleyball player than I ever imagined. I studied long and hard to keep myself from being ineligible with my grades. It was daunting and taxing on my body and mind. I had to study so much harder to keep up with the other students, but it was worth it because I never had to sit the bench. At that point in my life, I had many areas to be intentional about but my skills were a natural flow from within. Happy doing it is an understatement.

That year, I made MVP in my district for volleyball. I also placed 2nd in State for 800, 2nd in state for the 400 and 2nd in State for cross country.

My giftings in sports was undeniable. But my struggle in academics left me wanting. The imbalance in my life's achievement was a hole that needed to be filled and I felt it very deep in my soul.

Cory, my boyfriend in high school, was tall, dark, very dark, and handsome, every girl's dream. He was the star basketball player of one of our small schools in our districts. He went to a different private school from me. I was the best volleyball player in our district, so it only made sense that we should get together. Everything was fun and exciting at first, but Cory liked to have a lot of female friends which really meant he liked to cheat. I was genuine and proud of our relationship, and I looked forward to a change in that, got made me partially relaxed in the relationship. He would always make sure I knew he had been with prettier girls and it made me look so small and unworthy of him. I saw what he was doing to me as a challenge and I wanted to please him the more, even though I wasn't finding validation within me. He talked about how skinny I was and that I needed more shape. Fear began to grip my heart, the fear of losing him, the fear of being lonely, I gradually began to be uncomfortable with myself and my looks. His words began to rule me, I was naive and young, how could I have known that I was allowing the wrong words to get to me. Soon into our relationship, Cory began to pressure me about having sex with him, it was one time I was able to stand up to him and not allow him to have his way. I knew what it would mean to begin allowing him to have sex with me and I was not in any way ready for it. Many times, I explained to him how I wanted to stay pure for the Lord and how it was wrong to have sex before marriage. When I would explain why I could not have sex, he would just give me the cold shoulder. This attitude of his was one part of him I never loved seeing, I always wanted to avoid him giving me cold shoulders even if it meant going against my own desires. I did love having me person around me.

I hated this because my mother would always do this to me growing up when I upset her. It really hurts. I was also afraid that he would want to be with someone else. So, I gave in once, then twice. Bam! I was pregnant. Everything happened so fast and I shockingly kept asking myself how I allowed myself go so far to the extent of getting pregnant. For few weeks, it still looked like a nightmare to me. I had so much guilt and shame. I didn't know what to do. Cory had already graduated from high school and had left for basic training in the Army. I was to enter my senior year of high school. In a panic, I went to my job to speak with Roxanne, the owner of Texas Lady Spa. She was understanding and comforting but her help came in one of the weirdest ways anyone could imagine. She offered to pay for an abortion, so I didn't have to drop out of school. I accepted. I alleviated myself of the burden of being pregnant, but I could not find release from my guilt. As I tried to keep my secret away from people, I was always finding it hard to hide from God because it always seemed as if he followed me about asking me for something I didn't think I could give.

I wrote Cory to tell him what I had done. He responded with hurt and angry words because he wanted to keep the child. Not me. I tried to hide the fact that I had even had sex. After all, what would people think of me?

A couple of weeks later, Cory wrote back and asked me to marry him. I quickly responded with, "I don't think that's God's plan for my life."

I felt free and dove into church with plenty of lip service, but I was not repentant in my heart. I think I was more afraid people would find out. I wanted to be sorry, and I don't know if I was. What I did understand was that I was broken. I thought I could hide what I had done. I thought if I threw myself into God's work, he would overlook my sin of murder.

Spiritually, I felt there was a rift between God and me that I could not repair.

1991

Senior years, this should have been the greatest year of my life at this point. My talent for volleyball during my senior year in high school had diminished, and no one could understand why.

I continued to try to do good things, but nothing could repair the emptiness I felt.

8

Senior Year

The senior year jitters were fast enveloping all of my classmates from the last leg of my junior year up to the moment when we commenced our senior year, and it was all they could talk about. Everyone seemed to want to talk about what college they were writing to, and why they thought they fit in there. It would have been manageable for me had they ended there, but it went on to the courses they would major in, and how suitable it was for their big dream and ambition. But there I was, seated at the far end of the last row, trying to block out all of their voices. I had once heard that the best way to avoid decisions was to act like they were non-existent, so that was what I was trying to do.

However, it was funny that the more I tried to block them out, the more audible they became, every word accentuated into my being. NYU became the anthem at every corner I turned to, and it was just worse that every student had seemed to become the perfect counselor for their friends who occurred to have been confused as to what course they should major in. Questions like 'what school organization do you belong in? Is the Press club a place you feel you can express yourself? How about the science club?' sprung up all over the place, and I just wanted to scream out, 'How about me? All I know how to do is volleyball!'

And even that was beginning to fall apart.

It started after my abortion in my junior year and the guilt that was beginning to eat me like a cankerworm. I was so self-conscious walking down the hallway of my school, that it soon felt like everyone was out to get me. The room became smaller and there wasn't suddenly enough space for me to walk through, as every eye turned to stare at me. Maybe it was just my imagination coming to play, as there was no way the kids at school could have gotten news of my abortion and how much it had affected my life. It was guilt, plain and simple. But it was stuck to me like a second skin, and I doubted I would be able to get rid of it anytime soon.

Post-abortion, the only thing I could boast of, got affected, and it was like starting from scratch all over again. The only difference was that I couldn't find it in me to start over. Volleyball, which once seemed to be my safe place was gradually being swept away by a mistake I had made not so long ago, and I suddenly wished I could call it all back. Maybe then, I would remotely feel the urge to discuss college applications with the rest of my classmates and chuckle at those that seemed to be confused about what they wanted. But how could I, when I was stuck in the same place?

On the volleyball court, it took a while before I could relate easily with my teammates again, and the whole period I was trying to get rid of my shame and stop thinking about the little scar that remained somewhere inside of me, my skills deteriorated, and I was back to being yelled at by my coach. He tried to get across to me during each training when I looked lost in myself, but my shame was stronger than his will, and it soon became an almost impossible task.

I thought I had escaped the whole gist about college applications for about the next twelve hours, one sunny afternoon after the close of day. But I was only kidding myself as my mother unexpectedly brought it up during supper.

"My friends' kids all seem to have nothing more to talk about than college applications and essays," she began, taking a gulp from the glass of orange juice seated in front of her plate. It was one of those days she got in earlier than expected and seemed to want to catch up with what we had been up to. "But I have never heard you talk about any of it since you got into your senior year. Am I missing anything?"

I knew my mother would couch her question that exact way. It was subtle, yet pointed all hands to the fact that I never talked about my academics at home. She didn't want to be caught up with wasting her money on a child who didn't even value it and trust me, I understood. I totally did.

"Uhmmm," I said, clearing my throat. "I haven't thought about it yet." There was no essence of lying to my mother, as she was bound to find out in the end. It was just like the time I backed into Ms. Paker's car, and I pleaded with her not to tell my mother because I knew it could get me into serious trouble. Even though I appeared to be bothered about it at home, I thought my mother wouldn't find out since Ms. Paker was so kind to me, and had even taught me how to study. But one day, I returned home to my mother talking about a certain 1,000 dollars that I owed my teacher for backing into her car. Even though I didn't get into trouble because of the way my teacher had told my mother, and Ms. Paker had refused any form of monetary help, it still made me know that there was no hiding anything from my mother.

"And why is that Tyra?" She questioned, getting serious real fast.

I sat up quickly, knowing that I had been walking on eggshells since the end of my junior year, and any wrong move I made could turn on me. "I will do that soon."

Although I knew that wasn't the end of that conversation, my mother said nothing else, but instead moved on to my siblings to ask how they had been doing academically. It was her way of telling me to better have something tangible to say the next time she asked that question. But I also knew that she was seeking actions and not stories.

So, the next day in school, I paid a visit to a teacher, who I thought could be of help to me and my situation. She smiled warmly at me and even offered me a bottle of drink.

Maybe this was it, I thought to myself.

"So you don't think you are good enough to be considered being given a spot in any university?" She questioned, staring at me the way I believed a priest would stare at his parishioner during a confession. I didn't know for sure, but it was just the weird way my mind worked.

I shook my head in response. "I'm scared that I wouldn't make it in there and would have to return to my mother as a failure and big disappointment."

"But you have good grades, don't you?" The teacher asked rhetorically. "I've seen you quite a number of times on the volleyball court, and I know that for you to have been given the opportunity to play for the school in a major game, your grades must have been up to par, or at least, acceptable."

I nodded again, with my head trying to come up with the easiest way of conveying my fears to the teacher. "My skills have been dropping in recent times, and the coach is threatening to put me out on the bench."

"And why do you think that is?"

I almost breathed a sigh of relief, as we were finally close to what I have been trying to communicate. "I'm not smart academically, and I have had to struggle my way through. It's hard enough that volleyball made me want to study so I could be off the bench, but what if there is no volleyball in the college I get accepted into?"

"Dear child," the teacher said, coming around to sit beside me. "I want you to understand that everyone deserves a shot at education, irrespective of their chosen fields. You deserve to go to college, and you should never forget that. Away with your fears and the other things holding you back, just make a move and apply. Let's see where it ends."

I thought my head was going to fall off from the amount of nodding I was doing, but there was no other way to communicate I understood, without interrupting her.

"It is true that if you weren't sound academically in high school," the teacher continued. "there's a high chance that you would not cope in college as it is a whole different ball game out there. But you're smart, okay? And you are going to figure it out."

I wanted to ask what exactly I was going to figure out, but it seemed like a lot coming from me. My visit to the teacher, apparently, did more harm than good, because, at that moment, I was certain that colleges weren't for me. Although she was right about my academics, as I only made As and Bs, and occasionally one C, it still made no sense to me as I struggled to get those grades. It wasn't like volleyball as I did it with so much ease, and I was scared of having to do that in college, only to still fail at it.

But my mother needed a reply, and there was no way I was going to walk over to her and tell her I was scared of going to college and doubted I would ever be going. Even without doing it yet, I was assured of a very thorough scolding, and maybe a visit to a counselor. But at the end of the day, I would still have to write and submit an application right before her. And that would only have been worse.

So I decided to try my hands on a few colleges, but the ones I reached out to seemed to care more about my grades in high school than what I could offer the volleyball team. I had expected it, but not as much as the quality of responses I had been getting. It would have been fine to boast about my grades, but that would have meant these schools had a level of expectation from me; something I knew I couldn't meet up to. So it was best to tone it down, waiting for the most positive reply; something that gave me the chance to play volleyball for as long as I wanted to, while still not giving so much importance to grades.

But the most positive one was to practice and train with the college volleyball team for a year to build up my lost skills, and then get a scholarship the following year to ensure I meet up with the required grades so I could play officially in the team. But that was still a lot.

It took a long while for me to finally get my guilt tucked into the deepest part of my memory, and forge ahead with my future, but I did. I was in a fellowship at the close of the day one evening, when my youth pastor asked what my plans were for college. I was about to tell him the same thing I told my mother when he suggested I applied to a certain Bible college. Although it came as a rather surprising recommendation, given the fact that I felt like a fraud throughout my Christian exploits in that community, my youth pastor thought it was something I should consider exploring. He seemed to believe more in me.

I applied to the Bible college and got accepted, which came as another rude shock, as I expected my application to be ignored like the others I had applied to. My mother was glad that I at least, knew what I wanted. But I wished I could tell her that she was wrong, and I was very surprised about the development.

But I graduated after a year, based on the specifics of the program in the Bible college. And even at that moment, it still came as a surprise.

Houston, Texas 1995

I began going to clubs with friends in my early 20's. It was all so new and exciting! For the first time in my life, I got lots of attention from boys. The guys were all over me, cascading me on an ocean of flirtatious chatters, glances, and winks… as if daring me to take a bite, to chew as hard as I pleased. I felt almost attractive, added to the fact that my newly discovered hair weave was everything I wanted and more. It made loud statements, ones that I was pleased with. Or maybe I thought I was.

Growing up, I didn't get much attention from anyone, and it was more disappointing than I let on at the time. Still, nothing could have been done about it at that time. I came from a big family where everyone sought to be seen and heard, but after my mom became widowed, I was often overlooked and ignored, so much that I didn't recognize how lonely I was, and how I craved companionship and care. My mom worked long hours as a police officer to support us, coming in daily with fatigue and stress glaring on her face. As a result, she had limited time and leftover energy to spend time with each one of us individually. It would have been inconsiderate of me to demand attention, but I wasn't even thinking about it anymore. Maybe it was just my coping mechanism.

Since I was the oldest, household chores usually fell on me. All the dishwashing and house tidying wasn't an issue for me. I was a responsible teenager in most regards, wanting to show my tired-working mother that I was fine and that she had no reason to worry about me. But this was far from the case when it came to academics. I had concluded that school was definitely not for me a long time ago. I had been held back twice in elementary school, and every year up until eighth grade, I was in danger of being held back again. It was intriguing how that didn't seem to bother me after a while, as I was content investing in household chores and working out ways to be responsible without necessarily needing education.

Suddenly receiving so much attention at the club was a refreshing change; it was also something I wasn't used to. It was so enchanting because I wasn't even conscious of my innate desire for it. It made the new club scene wonderful and exciting, like a drug I couldn't get enough of. I wasn't scared of an overdose because I didn't believe in the possibility of that happening. Guys were genuinely interested in me, or so I thought. How was I expected to know they were more interested in what they could get from me and that neither of those things included a handshake or a silly dance routine? My already weak self-esteem allowed me to easily and quickly give them what they wanted, hands wide open in absolute surrender; and when they just moved on to the next piece of meat, I didn't care even for a minute because I was finally getting the attention, I discovered I craved.

At first, I went out only once a week. But as the months went by, the outsides saw me more often, with my naive and attention-deprived self, until I was going out four nights a week. It was a stunning discovery, knowing I could smile my way through to get what I needed, compared to waiting at home all day for the scraps of attention that still had to be shared by every member of the family. I was at it and doubted it could get any worse until it did.

On one of my nights at the club, a girl asked me, "Are you a dancer?"

"I took a few lessons when I was younger," I replied, wondering what direction she was heading with that question.

"No, girl, I am talking about topless dancing- a stripper." She seemed exasperated that I hadn't immediately understood what she meant.

I wasn't sure what to say, so I simply stammered a no. I was embarrassed that she even asked, as that was my first time being led to think about it. As she kept talking, I realized that the girl meant it as a compliment.

"Well, I'm Renee," she said, reaching for a handshake. Renee was a striking beauty, with piercing green eyes that could turn heads and a body that could keep them staring long after. "And I bet you could make a lot of money." She explained.

That got my attention. I had been waiting tables at a restaurant, but it wasn't fetching me as much money as I would have liked. Relying on such a meager wage, I could barely afford a place to live. So, I had to listen when Renee said she could help me figure out a way to end my monetary troubles. Later, I wondered if I would still have responded in a positive manner if Renee hadn't been so persistent. She began calling every day to see if I wanted to meet up again, inviting me to what was to become my favorite club.

It took her a couple more calls, but soon enough, we hit the club together. We became so close that people did not recognize us a part, though I wondered how that happened, since we had only been friends for a couple of months. One day, Renee got the idea that we should get an apartment together along with another friend of ours, Blanca. Of course, you can tell how we met Blanca too.

I had absolutely no problems with that. The prospect was fascinating, as I was finally going to be living in a place other than other people's couches. Can you picture it? Can you see the ambiance and warmth that was supposed to spring from that decision? Blanca and Renee did all the leg work in finding a place we could call home. A week later, I received a phone call from Renee that they had found the perfect apartment. The three of us, as single women and close companions, would live together in a spacious apartment right across the street from our favorite club, J. Larkins. I could feel it was going to be the best year ever. It was great living with two other girls who loved to live life to its fullest and whose spontaneous acts kept me wanting more of that life. Our after parties were epic, and I quickly became hooked on the lifestyle. I mean, what could have been more fun than that?

After about a month of eventful rooming with my girls, as I loved to call them, their behavior started to become odd and out of character. It began with the little conversations that seemed to leave me out and then the laughs I had no idea who it was directed to. There were also inside jokes that I never understood. I thought I was an insider too.

Many times, Blanca and Renee were alone in a room, talking with the door shut. I began to wonder what they were whispering about, a part of me afraid that it would be me. It began to piss me off, hearing their silent chuckles and whispers behind closed doors. One day, I decided to just walk in, demanding to know what they were up to. I found them inside the room, kneeling on the floor and sniffing a white powder with straws.

"Do you want some?" Blanca asked, not looking up to see who had just walked in. Of course, there would have been no need to since it was just the three of us who lived in the apartment. But still, I expected some form of a surprise that I was standing in front of them. But instead, it felt like they had been expecting me for a while now.

I just stared at them with my mouth hanging open in surprise. I hadn't expected the scene that had greeted me.

"No, thanks," I answered, shaking my head as if to reiterate my rejection. I could see that they were very nervous about what I would think. It was as if, although they had expected me to find out somehow, they still weren't sure how I would feel about it.

They were right to have been nervous, as I was shocked because I had never seen actual cocaine before. My fight or flight kicked in, and I quickly left the room, deciding to protect what little sanity I had left. It was funny. I hadn't thought about how long that decision would keep me.

After those few minutes in that room, I tried pushing the entire incident to the back of my mind. I chose to act like it never happened and was relieved that it hadn't turned out to be what I feared. They had both been keeping something from me, but it wasn't to spite me or anything like that. Later that night at the club, everyone was feeling really lovey-dovey.

Renee kept saying, "I am wiggin'. I am wiggin' girl," with her eyes rolling back in her head. She seemed to be very happy, her grin spread wide over her flushed face.

I asked, "What is Wiggin?" I felt stupid saying the word out loud, but I couldn't help it.

| A REWRITTEN STORY

Completely surprised by the question, Renee looked at me as if I had just asked something so strange, maybe the most bizarre in the History of Strange Questions. She laughed and said, "You don't know what Wiggin is? You've heard of Ecstasy, right?" She arched her head sideways, studying me so intently that I felt like I was about to fall below some standard.

"Nope," I said, trying to sound as casual and non-nonchalant as possible.

"You have to try it," she said with a glint in her eyes. Renee loved taking on new experiments, and I was sure I had felt like one at that moment.

"It's not a *hard* drug." She explained, sensing my distress.

"Na, girl, I don't do drugs." I always remained firm in that stance.

"You can't get addicted to it because it's a pill." Renee was trying hard to get me to see reason, and a part of me feared I was doing just that.

"Really?" I questioned, trying to tell my rational self that drugs were different from a pill, their difference being the distinct ability to cause an addiction. Maybe addiction was what I truly feared.

"You'll love it. I'll get you one!" Renee's voice was laced with excitement, the type that came after a success. "Trust me. It's better to do it with a group. Then, you'll have much more fun when it sets in."

I had to admit that Renee's confidence convinced me that the risks of getting addicted were slim. Or maybe convincing me wasn't as hard as I had thought. Either way, there I was, considering doing something I had so hated only a year ago. Like most people who have never tried drugs, I worried about getting addicted. But if what Renee said was true, what did I have to lose?

Nothing!

Absolutely nothing!

I eventually gave in, trying the pill with the people I shared a special bond with. I would have loved to tell you that it was a bad experience, but unfortunately, I can't. It was great! It made me happy, like I suddenly had no problems in the world. I imagined I was at home, sitting on my favorite couch, watching my mother stretch her tired limbs before asking how my day had gone. I also imagined I was in the arms of someone who loved me, showering me with all the attention I deserved. I was chuckling so hard at his jokes and stares. But it had all been a dream. I had known it, but oh, how real it felt! Must have been something extra in the pill.

The comedown, however, was horrible.

With stimulants like cocaine and Ecstasy, your serotonin and dopamine levels get higher than usual, giving you the same feeling as being in love. When the body starts to come down, it wants the peak again. So, a person will dose herself again, though it is nearly impossible to regain the original high. With each comedown, the low feels worse than the one before because you have interfered with the normal functioning of serotonin producers and receptors in your brain.

The comedown is what encourages people to do whatever it takes to get high again. My first experience with drugs was so good that I had to try it again just to make sure that I liked it as much as I remembered. I did, but I still hated the comedown. Ecstasy would keep me so wired on the comedown that I couldn't sleep a wink; I would be up all night hoping another pill would magically drop out of the sky. I wish I could have foreseen that opening this door would cost me years of suffering. But I kept experimenting with drugs, starting a cycle that led to more pills every weekend. It was a jumbo of highs and comedowns, but in everything, I felt a newfound devotion to something other than trying to make money and gain attention.

At the time, I didn't see anything wrong with it. After all, I still had the power to turn down my roommates when they offered me a line of cocaine. That made me feel proud, like I wasn't totally losing control. There was an increase in my level of confidence, knowing that I knew how to handle and maintain my stuff. It was something the girls in the club worked on, subtly showcasing their prowess in taking drugs without making a fool out of themselves. I found it easier than most of them, giving me a false sense of confidence.

I continued this clubbing cycle with my exciting new friends for about a year. It was from one table to another, one man to another, one bed to the next. The demands were as exciting as their prospects.

One month during my newly discovered lifestyle exploitation, Renee was short on rent. This wasn't even the first time it had happened. It was funny that we were so short on money at that time. Maybe our drug addiction problem was partly to blame, but no one was going to consciously think about that, of course.

Renee got the bright idea to go and strip at a club to make money. The thought appalled me, creating images in my head of poles, crowds, and the danger. But Renee, being herself, managed to convince me to accompany her, soothing my worries with the one thing I had come to value: Friendship.

"If you were my friend, you would do this with me," she said, her beautiful eyes drawing me into a pool of emotions. I knew it was an appeal to emotion, but there was no way I was going to refuse.

I really was Renee's friend. She had been there for me the whole time we had lived together, helping me get through my difficult times and showing me the ropes of all I needed to know. She was always nice to me. I decided it was my turn to be Renee's good friend, as there was no better way I could pay her back.

I agreed to go to the strip club, but only for support.

Renee and I entered the cold, dark club, and I instinctively wrapped my arms around myself, trying to ward off the sudden chill. I had dreaded going, but now that I was here, I was even more fearful. I didn't think I could pull it off. The dancers at J. Larkin where we hung out were all beautiful and sexy. I thought there was no way I could pull the amount of attention I would need, at least not as much as Renee would with those enchanting eyes and scintillating body.

Renee asked to see the manager. She flexed her beautiful curves without care. In my self-delimitation, I noticed that the men in the club were staring at me. I was still debating about whether to return to the car or not when a waitress pointed to the owner of the club, a white-haired man with a white goatee, who also wore a white suit. There was a lot of white going on.

Oddly enough, his name was Whitey. How convenient. Renee introduced us with an enviable self-assurance. I suddenly wished I had half of the confidence she had, as that would at least spare me from thinking about how inadequate I was for this. Whitey said he would have to see us in our G-strings before we could be hired. I didn't even own a G-string. In fact, I was wearing my granny panties.

My mind began racing. Something inside me was telling me that this wasn't right and would only lead to more problems. When I told Whitey that I wasn't wearing a G-string, I secretly hoped it would blow my chances.

Then I could tell Renee that I had at least tried to be the good friend she had wanted at that moment, but that it hadn't been up to me. But Whitey said it was okay, that he just needed a look at my body to see if he liked what he saw. He added that the club had a high set of standards; for a second, I was sure I wouldn't meet that standard.

This did not help with the butterflies in my stomach at all.

After Whitey's careful evaluation, I surprisingly found myself with a new job. Weirdly enough, Renee was rejected because she had tattoos on her legs. It didn't make any sense to me, because there was a considerable margin between mine and Renee's looks, but Whitey was determined to stand by his decision. It caused Renee to give me the cold shoulder for a whole week. I guess she felt like I was stealing something she had really wanted; to sort out the house bills as well as adequately fend for herself. But how would I have explained to her that I was clueless about what happened with Whitey's evaluation and had even tried chipping in a word for her?

After weighing the pros and cons, I finally decided that I could really use the money to pay for my attempt at college. Giving it a try sounded like the best option for me. Strip club, here I come!

Thinking about my first-time dancing on the stage that night still scares me. I was so nervous that I could feel my legs shaking as I mounted the linoleum podium of the club. I wasn't sure if anyone would like me, with my small curves and my hair that never seemed to straighten out no matter how hard I tried. I had high hopes of men coming up and throwing piles of bills on the stage for me. Up on stage, the lights were bright, casting a glow on the faces of a small portion of the watching audience. It was worse that way, being able to see their every expression and thoughts about each dancer's performance. My nervousness set in again, threatening to ruin the night for me. Should I move right? Or left? Should I lift both arms or arch my back in a seductive manner instead? At that point, I was not sure I could even remember how to dance, so I just began to move. At least it was a start. A huge one for me.

The other areas of the stage were so brightly lit that one couldn't see into the faces of the audience. This was a blessing in disguise for me. If the bright lights kept me from discovering what the men in the audience thought of me, then I couldn't be happier! But it didn't shield the expressions of the few that I could see, with their suggestive winks and acknowledging nods.

On the first night, I didn't know what other strippers thought of their audience, but I concentrated mainly on making sure I wouldn't trip on stage, falling flat on my face onto the ground, and becoming a laughingstock. I had no time to wonder whether the guys would be able to identify me when I was outside of the club and going about my daily activities or what would cause them to notice me here in the club. That first song seemed to last forever, and I just wanted it to end.

When I finally got offstage and counted the money that had been tucked into my short dress, I realized I had made a measly four dollars. All that stress and worry brought me ... *just four dollars!* It made me feel terrible.

A petite girl named Chocolate saw me crying and approached me. She immediately understood my troubles, stating that she had the same issues when she initially started out in the club. She told me I needed to do table dances to make real money. She asked me to look around for them and notice the difference between both dances. Sure enough, when I wiped my tears and looked up, I saw a girl dancing above a man who almost looked in pain. In fact, he was so eager to be close to the dancing girl's body that it almost seemed to hurt him to refrain from doing so. It was a stunning contrast, and I couldn't help but stare.

Men were allowed to touch the women at this club but tried to avoid doing it. I guess their reason was to keep their minds from criticizing them but rationalize their actions since they weren't technically cheating on their wives. I seriously wondered how I would be able to deal with this.

Chocolate told me I had to go and ask the men if they wanted a dance. If they said yes, I would have to charge them no less than twenty dollars a dance.

So, what did I do with Chocolate's advice?

Nothing.

I just sat alone because I was too shy to walk up to random men and ask them if they wanted me to dance for them. It sounded too unbecoming to me, and I know it shouldn't have, considering the fact that I was employed in a club. That alone was already saying much. But still, I couldn't do it.

Later that night, two men came up to me and asked me to dance for them. It felt safer that way, knowing that I hadn't had to walk up to their table to request it. What if they had ended up turning me down?

I danced for both men, nervous and scared. The problem was that the men were touching me. I couldn't seem to get with that. I wasn't ok and I felt out of control. On my first night, I made forty-four dollars. That was a little more than I was making waiting tables. But still, I wanted to quit dancing, as everyone else made hundreds of dollars in that one night. And I could only make just this much. Maybe the whole dancing stuff wasn't for me, just as I had believed, in my younger years, that education wasn't for me.

When I went home, my roommates encouraged me to keep trying. "You can't give up after one week," they argued, with Renee already over the rejection at the club. "You have 40 more dollars than you would have had". It was a logical assumption.

So, I continued to go every day for the next couple of weeks and kept coming home with $40 because I was too afraid to ask anyone for a dance. I did not know I was shy. But Fridays were better, as I came home with $100. On Monday through Thursday, I made $40 a night and $100 on Fridays.

This went on for a month before it hit me. If I try a different club, I might have better luck. There was something about the consideration of location and ambiance that my economics teacher had said while I was in high school. I wasn't sure what the details of her lecture had been, but I knew it would prove helpful here. I was told about a club named Fantasy where touching was prohibited, and the girls made a lot of money, but men were not allowed to touch them.

I went there, as skeptical about my being accepted as I had been the first time. But there was no need for that. It was a success as more guys asked me to dance, and they paid much better. I was making about $200-300 on a slow night and $500-1500 on the weekends. For a while, I was the highest-paid girl in the club.

I was elated. I had saved an admirable amount of money, and so I finally decided to attend San Jacinto College. I eventually joined the college, but the late hours at Fantasy led to poor class attendance and low grades, so I had no choice but to drop my courses.

During my time there, I made friends with the head of the psychology department, who feared that if I dropped out of college, I might never return.

I did not want to think about this, but it weighed heavily on my mind.

I continued to dance, and I made a lot of money in my first year. Then one night, I went to The Gold Cup as a favor to a friend; this was a higher-class club. The building was beautiful on the outside, with flowers lining the sidewalk and beautiful lighting that produced a variety of colors.

However, no one ever warned me that you could go to jail for doing something legal. Maybe if I had known, I wouldn't have been at that club that night. Just maybe.

Oblivious to me, I danced for an undercover officer and set myself up for absolute failure – I landed in jail.

I called my mother to let her know that I had gotten arrested, because I was afraid that she might end up being the one to take my fingerprints if they transferred me to the county jail. It was better to give her the unpleasant news myself.

"Hi, Mom ... I've something to tell you." I stammered through the words, wanting to get it out fast but seeming unable to. "I am in jail."

"Why are you in jail?" Her voice sounded confused, like she thought I was pulling a prank on her.

"Public lewdness," I answered.

"Tyra, I don't believe it." She scoffed, and I could hear her relax a little. At that moment, I wished she was right, that I wasn't such an abject failure that dragged her tired self-up from bed in a bid to protect her failing child.

That comment rang in my ear for a while. I would like to say that I wised up right away after that. The tone of my mother's voice indicated that I had disappointed and even hurt her. I didn't want to hurt her; I wanted her approval, like most children. But I had started a lifestyle that I had grown accustomed to; quitting now would render me financially disabled.

Amidst all this dancing away, making money, joining college, leaving college, going to jail, and everything else in between – God was always at the back of my mind. I don't positively mean this. He was in my mind entirely for different reasons. I was sure He didn't care much about me anymore because I had turned my back on Him.

I had disobeyed Him, so why would He help me now? Even while such thoughts plagued my mind, a little part of me told me a different story. It said to me that He is still there, calling out to me even if all my sins had landed me in jail.

Days turned into weeks, and I was locked in myself, trying to make sense of all that was happening, wondering if I could ever lead a life without the things, I had grown accustomed to.

My mother called me a couple of weeks after I got out of jail.

"Hi, I just wanted you to know that I love you," she calmly said, and I could hear the smile in her voice. "The Lord has not forgotten about you." Her call warmed my heart and made my eyes well up with tears. After we hung up, I kept replaying the conversation in my mind. Maybe it was a sign that He still loved me?

I wasn't ready yet to leave this life I'd made, but knowing God was still there felt good. I had never really meant much to anyone. I was always second to someone else, or just not enough. As a dancer, I knew that people thought me attractive and unique, even if it was just for one night of lights and music.

But I felt that there was something more for me, I just couldn't seem to place my hands on it. Maybe I would have asked God, but I didn't even know how to communicate with him without letting go of the guilt plaguing my mind.

I was a mess. A crooked one.

10

Trafficked

Firsts things first! You should never confuse a stripper with a prostitute. A high majority of the prostitutes are trafficked, but some are not. Although they may seem the same as a dancer, they are entirely different things. Girls who are trying to get ahead will dance; girls without any hope will prostitute or are modern day slaves whom who are trafficked.

Having firsthand experience with being a dancer, I realized that there are many things that people don't understand about strippers and strip clubs. The people who go to the clubs don't talk about why they go or what happens there. More so, strippers do not spend their free time explaining to people how they pay their bills or how hard it is getting by without having to be ostracized by society, including those inside the clubs.

To understand me and my story, I should probably explain a few things about the complex lives of strippers, prostitutes, the human trafficked, customers, and strip clubs.

Strippers are a strange and rare breed, so much so you can only pick them out of a line-up if they are dancing, for say at a regular old dance club. Most dancers love the attention that comes with the job and being listened to, but they are also excellent listeners. They are not always starved for attention. Sometimes the attention could get overwhelming, drawing them into a swamp of unnecessary actions. A dancer making money and getting plenty of attention is having both her material and emotional needs met simultaneously. A form of closure comes with it, albeit an illusion. Their emotional needs cease to be met when they stop being the exact way the men require, or if the cycle begins. Although the attention is intoxicating sometimes finding true love is much harder to come by.

However, this is an ugly cycle because every dancer has nights where they are not compulsorily seen and felt at work. Nothing is more devastating to a dancing girl's ego than going to work and realizing that no one is interested in her that night, or even worse, throughout that week. During such times, past feelings of rejection and abandonment will rear their head, dragging the individual into the re-awakened aura of the past. The false sense of emotional satisfaction is lost, and then it becomes evident that it is all an illusion. Although, this doesn't stop the girls from coming back and relentlessly trying again. It is a cycle, and a resulting fantasy is better than the feeling of emptiness.

But for me, dancing gave me the confidence that I once lacked. I became more daring and challenging, even if it was far from the point where I was coming from.

I was raised in a culturally diverse area. We were taught to respect, or at least pretend to respect one another outwardly, regardless of any differences we may quietly perceive. Most of the people I encountered up until this point in my life acted the same way. My neighborhood was a nicer lower middle class suburban one, and I had no problems but used to not quite fitting in. Toleration was not an issue there, as everyone felt the people around them deserved some level of acknowledgment. Until I began dancing, I felt discrimination was not a massive issue for people of my generation and background. But the truth is that I only had this thought because I was in a cloak for a long time. It became more apparent the moment I stepped out.

At a strip club, racial issues are out in the open and never brushed aside in the name of "good manners." Some nights, people did not want me to dance for them because I didn't have blonde hair or blue eyes. Those days were the few times I wished there was an issue with my lineage, where I would suddenly develop the features of a soft American, and my mother would suddenly declare that I was adopted. Other nights, people only wanted me because they had some crazed fantasy about African American girls. And I never thought about being white at those times. I wondered if the white dancers ever wished they were black. The strip club is all about fantasies: fulfilling and recreating. Dreams of how people think things are and how they wish they could be. But just like all fantasies, when reality dawns, it shocks one into a state of disbelief. So here, the critical factor in surviving is the awareness that everything is nonexistent. Well, apart from the money.

A man who comes into a strip club is looking to have this fantasy fulfilled, to have some perception reinforced, or to get the attention he is not getting elsewhere. When a man walks into a club, he can finally get any girl he wants to dance with – that is the illusion that the dancers give as they vie for customers to pay them for dances. They present themselves as affordable and achievable, doing everything and anything within their power to make these men feel powerful under those beautiful dark lights. They compete for the men's money, but the men tell themselves that the dancers are competing for them. It always turns out that both sides know it goes no further than a dance and perhaps a snippet of conversation if the lady is witty enough. Most times, all they want is to dance, get paid, and walk out of there with the few shreds of dignity they have left. Who gives a damn about you trying to tell me how your day went?

The only potential downside for a man coming to a strip club is if he doesn't have any money. As they say, "No money, no honey." They are treated like people with some terminal disease, getting avoided by all the girls available for the night. Their faces are also marked and recognized by the girls, so as to warn the newbies of their financial illness and possible communicable state. Even then, the idea of a beautiful woman flirting and acting interested may be enough to bring him satisfaction. Emphasis on maybe.

A strip club sells a fantasy, and the men are happy to buy it all up. Whether it is the stripper herself or the men on the other side, everyone knows that none of it is real.

What is the one quality that a stripper needs to have a lucrative career? Most would say that she needs impressive dancing skills. And I agree. I mean, if she doesn't know how to dance, what will she do up on stage? Juggle?

I don't think so.

But for a girl seeking to make a living as a stripper, there's something even more important than dancing – incredible acting skills.

In order to fulfill the fantasy, a successful dancer must also be trained as a believable actress. Maybe a new dancer naively believes that dancing is enough to make money. Girls who have stayed longer know that they aren't just paid to dance. Think about it: hopping on a stranger's lap, pretending that the hideous creature is handsome – despite his bad breath, receding hair line, and big gut – convincing him to part with $20 for just four minutes of your time, after which you will move ten feet away to the next heinous man and do it all over again. It is a cycle that goes further than a mere dance on the stage in front of ogling eyes.

You need pretty good "faking it" skills to do this effectively. And it is so challenging pretending to be interested in a man who is anything but appealing to you. Sometimes, you have to ignore their body odors, stemming from a tedious day at work, or even their unappealing personalities just so you can take something home for the night.

So, I did – I learned the skills of acting, at least well enough to convince the customers in the strip club. I wasn't perfect, but it got me what I desired. On some nights, there just wasn't enough money in the world, and I knocked the heck out of a few guys who touched me. My rule was to look but never touch.

However, I learned to mask my emotions pretty well overall – not the best skill to have as a woman of faith, as it makes it easier to hide from yourself and your own emotions as well, because your emotions are the most potent adversary that stands against in this line of occupation.

I would be lying if I didn't mention that a lot of girls who become dancers have been hurt in some way, mentally or physically. It's common for a girl who has been raped or molested or maybe has suffered some abuse or neglect to become a dancer. They have already developed some masking and hiding skills, and they have also dealt with men touching them the wrong way. Theirs may even take a whole new turn, as the act of their being touched the wrong way happened in such a brutal and vengeful manner that recovering from that takes more than the sympathetic glances that come with it. I have known fellow dancers whose mother or father sold their virginity for drugs or money. At the time, I was too self-absorbed to realize it, but it's easier for a dancer to rationalize the poor treatment at the club, if all you have ever known is poor treatment.

At least in the club, you're getting paid for it. So, it makes your job of "putting on a show" seem worthwhile.

Being a dancer is about being able to control your environment and the men in it. This is another reason damaged women work in strip clubs – it offers a sense of control that is otherwise missing in their daily lives. A strip club is the best place for a woman to try to exert control over a man. In the club, I was able to have a certain amount of power, albeit a false sense of control. It is almost always an illusion.

In fact, the male customer likely has a wife at home; almost all of them either told me they had wives or were in a committed relationship. The stripper has no control over a man who answers to another woman, even if she is sitting on his lap. He will tell you how great and beautiful his wife is, yet he is paying to have you coo and fuss all over him. How much control is that?

Men like to believe that they've still got it no matter what – sex appeal, attractiveness, whatever causes women to chase men. So, they take a chance and gamble with their families and their relationships with their wives because they feel they will always be taken back if they are ever caught. I guess they feel like they aren't really cheating since they're not actually having sex. Well, I believe, and I think most women would agree, that this is cheating. More importantly, touching a naked woman who is not your wife is worth a death sentence to your marriage. Some men I met in a strip club were incredibly unattractive; I could never take them seriously. Now and then, a lovely gentleman would venture into the club, so perhaps we ought to give him the benefit of the doubt. But what kind of man voluntarily steps into a strip club? Maybe they are the unmarried ones in search of a warm body to make them feel less lonely. Or perhaps they are just plain interested in the dance, excited to see the accentuated curves move and wiggle unashamedly on the dance floor, garnering the attention of everyone that dared to look for even a second. That could be why this set of individuals continues to return after that first experience. But still, it doesn't send a good message about his lifestyle. Well, neither does being a stripper/ dancer.

Hustler – that is a word that would definitely describe a dancer. They are relentless in getting a reasonable amount of money by the end of every night, sometimes regardless of how it is earned. While you might find a hustler at any place, you are sure to find a bunch of them at a strip club. These girls have to become very inventive to convince a man to come up with $20 for a four-minute dance. It doesn't take much to convince a man who willingly walked into a strip club to watch a dance for that amount. But it is still a lot of hard work, as these men love it when ladies act sneaky for something they want, even if they never admit it.

Strippers would make great stockbrokers, used-car salespeople, and pharmaceutical sales individuals. These women can probably sell anything, as the trickiest part of the concept of trade has been learned in a skimpy dress and a room with blue and red lights. A stripper closes the deal, makes her money and gets the job done – usually in four minutes or less. She thinks about it sometimes, probably on her way back from the strip club or even while at home. Condemnation and guilt cease to make their way in after a while because it isn't hard justifying every act.

Dancers are very straightforward; if they think it, they have already said it. Every one of their clients is expected to keep up. This is the strange nature of strippers: some of the most beautiful women all in one place, dressed to the T, spewing the most horrific words through their lips. The mouth of a stripper is more shocking than a sailor's mouth on any given night. This has been one of the most challenging habits to get rid of long after I left the strip club and moved into the professional world. No matter how strong, my faith doesn't make it any easier for me to shut my mouth when I stub my toe! Imagine spewing out a disgusting curse word in the office when a colleague mistakenly takes the last granola bar, the one I had been saving with my name on it, without asking. I tend to forget about restitution and change at that moment, sometimes throwing all caution to the wind. However, God has done an amazing work on me.

In addition to saying exactly what you think without running it through a filter, there is another unwritten rule of dancing: territory. When a new girl comes in, she better stick to the rules and stay away from the other girls' repeat customers, or she will have a bunch of five-inch heels sticking out of her back. If a regular girl gets into a fight with a new girl, all the girls in the club will jump the new girl, and the new girl never returns. Inside the club, a gang mentality prevails where acts of meanness can seem perfectly normal. So, it is like an ideal place for teaching a craft or skill, where the existence of seniors who had been there before you must be acknowledged and considered. Whatever happens outside of this has the new girl to blame, regardless of the point of ignorance. Learning the ropes and learning it fast is one of the essential requirements of strip dancing.

As crazy as the whole world of stripping sounds, there is only one reason a girl becomes a dancer in the first place: money. I earned a lot of money dancing at least for a young girl, and before I got into drugs, I was able to live a fabulous lifestyle on my income. If you play your game well, you might even be lucky enough to find someone who foots your bills because he thinks he has something in it for himself. Remember, men love to believe they are all this and all that. If a girl can keep her nose clean (literally), she can usually save a lot of money. The problem for me was that I wasn't able to keep my head straight and my nose clean.

The things I had to do to make money turned me into something so hideous on the inside that I couldn't keep my faith or morals. I lost myself to the sin, the glamour, the greed.

I traded in my morals for what? Absolutely nothing.

Now, let's talk about the prostitute. These were girls that I refused to really associate with. Actually, I think many undersold themselves. The value of what they were offering was more than what they were selling it for.

This world and all the lights it come with a very dark side. It has taken me years to understand what I saw in the clubs and to understand the other side that existed in the dark. As a young girl I did not understand the world of human trafficking-slaves. I was always boggled by the fact that girls would dance and then give her money away to usually a man. I would ask sometimes "why". And the answer would be because he will beat us.

There were times I say girls come into the club that had been freshly beaten I did understand that getting involved would mean certain death at times. There were a couple occasions that I offered reuse and the girl declined with an "I can't". I was then cornered by the pimp and given a strong warning to mind my own business. No, I could never understand until I met Angelica. She was 17. The club owner's wife loved to sleep with her.

Angelica told me the story of how she became a dancer. "When I was 12 years old, I was on my own. A pimp took me in. One day When he was done with me, he let all his friends rape me, beat me, and they through me in a ditch left me for dead. I survived and I have been taking care of myself ever since".

My mind could not wrap itself around what I had just heard. Twelve years old. Why was she on the streets at twelve? I didn't ask. However, Angelica had a severe drug pill problem. The girl could take seven at Xanex at one time and it would be like nothing.

11

Traumatized

After getting arrested, you would think I would have been smart enough to see my life's direction and probably stopped dancing, but that did not happen.

I had never been a quitter and was not going to become one now, even when all the signs in the universe were trying to tell me that it was the best thing to do.

Immediately after getting out of jail, I was afraid of being arrested again, so I stopped dancing for a while. I couldn't stick to it, though, and went back soon enough – mainly because of the money. I couldn't have been blamed at this point because survival was an ingrained virtue throughout my days as a strip dancer. There was no way I would have been able to stay put until another means of sustainable livelihood strolled by, meeting me in the pools of debts and lack. I needed the money, and I went for it.

There weren't any jobs out there for a girl like me, none that paid that well. I had been dancing for a year, moving from man to man, trying to make them see the reasons why I was the best dancer for them each night. At this point I was still mostly drug free and just a social drinker although I was using Ecstasy on weekends, I didn't do cocaine and I didn't want to. I would dance, I told myself, but I would know where to draw the line.

One night there was a phone call in the locker room from someone who was looking for a dancer to perform at a party for a hundred dollars. For some reason, no one else wanted to do it, so I hastily jumped at the opportunity. I told the man on the phone that $100 would only buy 15 minutes of dancing plus tips. We exchanged phone numbers, and I got directions from the man on the phone. I headed out alone, thinking it would be just another regular frat house party of young boys wanting quick entertainment. I should have made more inquiries before jumping at the opportunity. I didn't even take into consideration that the other girls rejected the job for a reason I wasn't aware of. Angelica who never really talked a whole lot mumbled said, "you probably shouldn't go". I chalked it up to her being high.

"One hundred dollars for 15 minutes I got this. I'll be back as soon as I'm done". I had recently decided that I needed a new car so I was going to make as much as I could as fast as I could,

When I got to the house where the party was supposed to be, it was little more than a shack, with peeling outside paneling and the outside smelt of dead rats. It was just a small white house in desperate need of a paint job and maybe thorough fumigation too. It was dark in front of the nondescript house, and there weren't any lights outside. As I walked up to the entrance to knock on the door, I kept hoping that nothing was lying on the ground that could make me trip and hit my head. Or worse, a puddle in the middle of the driveway. I couldn't make out a thing from where I was standing. Although from the driveway, I could see parked cars behind the house, presumably belonging to people at the party. Maybe it was because there was a florescent light at that part of the house, but probably purposely positioned to only provide a soft glow to that area.

The man who opened the door was not particularly tall, maybe five foot seven, with dark, curly hair springing up all over his head. It was so attractive that I felt like running my hands through it. He looked like he worked out a lot, with solid muscles visible from his tight shirt. He introduced himself as Jared, grinning from ear to ear at my appearance. I thought he looked excited to see me.

But there was no one else in the house. I remember thinking it didn't look like much of a party, as there wasn't even music or disposable red cups. I could have been working at the club for all I cared. I needed a new car and wanted to earn enough for a decent down payment. I was starting to get a little pissed realizing that this party had not begun yet.

"Is this the house for the party?" I asked Jared. He blinked twice as if taken by surprise, then nodded slowly, flashing his multi-dollar grin.

No, it was just him. I should have gotten the clue.

"Come on in. Let me get your money," Jared said, walking ahead of me. I sauntered behind him, following him into a room that looked like it was decorated in the late 70s. There was this damp smell, a click-clack of a big pendulum clock leaning beside a dresser, and curtains that did the nothing to flatter the space. Jared waited by the door until I stepped in, locking it almost immediately after me. The more I looked around, the more I needed this dance to be over with. We were still dancing, right?

"It's only a 15-minute dance," I told him, hovering close to the door. "That's fine," he said, handing me the money. "We talked about it on the phone, remember?"

"Where is everybody?" I asked again, noting the way his eyes shot up for the second time that night. "I thought this was a party. Do you have any music?" I didn't think to bring a radio. I didn't know bringing radios to a party was a thing.

"The others didn't show up," he said, angling his head as if studying me intensely. "Go ahead and dance. Show me what I paid for."

"I need music." I was beginning to get creeped out by the sudden silence enveloping the room. It was just the two of us, with old, outdated décor all around. I should have walked out. I know I should have. Usually, the girls at the strip club brought along a bodyguard for protection and to instill fear, but that night was on such short notice that I didn't have time to prepare anything. And besides, it was only going to be 15 minutes.

He reached into his dresser and brought out a wrapped paper. There was no sense in asking him what was in it as he put out a line of cocaine and asked, "Do you want some?"

"No thanks," I replied, shivering at the thought of doing cocaine with a total stranger.

"Let's do the dance now. I have to get back to the club." That wasn't a lie, even if I said it because I was getting scared to my bones. I still needed to make more money that night.

"Go ahead," he said, looking at me like I was a snack. I took off my quartz watch and placed it on the table where Jared had sniffed his lick of cocaine. I was always nervous around cocaine, knowing what it could cause to my thinking pattern at any instant.

Trying to contain my fear, I slowly danced near him in awkward silence, moving like I was back at the club, with a thousand pairs of eyes on me. I slowly took off my clothes until nothing was left except my T-back. I began to dance around him and on him, keeping my eyes on the quartz. Time seemed to go by even slower when there was no music, as I felt like I had been dancing for up to an hour. Then suddenly, Jared grabbed me by my arms, pulled me close, and forced me onto the second couch with one of his legs behind mine. He climbed on top of me and pushed my legs apart, smiling the whole time like someone who was without a conscience.

I managed to kick him off of me and immediately ran to the door, beads of sweat already adorning my face. But the door was dead-bolted, and the key wasn't in the keyhole anymore. I could have sworn I had seen it there when I stepped into the room earlier. I stood frozen, realizing I'd been locked inside the house. I tried hard to kick in my survival instinct, but it seemed to have abandoned me when I needed it the most. Maybe it had something to do with the amount of fear I felt in that moment. I couldn't even hold a thought for more than a second.

Jared got off the couch and slowly sauntered towards me, seeing that I had realized that I was stuck in there with him. He pulled me roughly to him when he got close enough, slamming his tongue in my ear. I fought back with all I had, knowing I couldn't allow him to have his way. While we struggled, Jared's elbow banged against my left temple, disorienting me as he dragged me back to his yellow paisley couch by the hair.

"Stop!" I yelled, even if a voice in my head reminded me of how deserted the driveway had looked. "Get off of me! This is not why I'm here!" I slapped at him and tried to loosen his grip on my hair weave. "Please stop! This is not why I'm here!" I tried again when I got no positive response, digging my feet into the carpet to resist. But my struggles were in vain.

Eventually, he got me to the sofa, forcing me onto my stomach. I could not believe what was happening, that I was getting raped and could do nothing about it. I kept fighting. I wasn't going to give in. In those awful minutes, my mind had gone completely numb. The more I struggled, the more excited he became. There was no use putting up a struggle anymore. No one was coming to save me. Finally, Jared finished and turned me around, licking and kissing my face. I was sick to my stomach.

Jared bent down to do another line of coke, leaving me on the couch without a second thought, like a used rag tossed aside. He pulled a pouch out from under the sofa, blithely going about his business. Like a robot, I rose slowly and padded across the small room to get my top, still clad in my T-back. I guess Jared had been too excited to take that off. I picked up my skirt, shaking all over. I could not control it.

"Come back over here and sit," Jared ordered, not bothering to look up at me. "We're not done partying." I felt sick just having to hear his voice. On my way back to the sofa, I noticed a key on a small coffee table next to the recliner where I first began dancing. That had to be the key to the front door, if my memory served me right.

I sat down obediently, without being able to put on my shoes. Jared reached under the sofa, pulled out another baggie, and threw it at me. I took the pouch and placed it inside my top. An hour or two ago at the club, I was excited to go to this "party" – thinking I would just do what I do every night: dance for money. But here I was, a *freaking victim*. He raped me and paid me to do it. This had been a setup straight from the beginning. Everyone must have known it but me. That must have been why the other girls refused to take the job. That was why I was the only one who indicated interest. There was nothing I could do about it.

Up to that point, I had never touched cocaine. I had limited myself to Ecstasy and Crown Royal because I thought I could control myself that way. But now, everything had changed. My world had been thrown off balance by one wrong decision.

I snapped back to reality when Jared told me he had to go to the restroom.

"When I come back, we're going to party again," he said, grinning again. I wished I could wipe that look off his face.

"So, you're going to rape me again," I said with disdain and fear. "This... is this what you call a party?"

Jared chuckled, grabbed one of my boobs, and licked my neck and ear. I wanted to throw up.

As soon as Jared left, I grabbed my purse and the key I noticed a few minutes ago, praying it was the right one. The door opened noiselessly, and I carefully shut it behind me. My heart was pounding so hard. I did not know if I would make it out alive. I looked behind me a million times, expecting Jared to suddenly jump out of the darkness and drag me back to that horrible room. He never did. I sped out of the driveway; glad I had left the keys in my car. Out on the highway, my hands shook on the steering, and I veered off the road several times as a result.

I was still shaking when I walked into the club, one of the safest zones for me at the moment. I went to the bathroom immediately to look in the mirror, wanting to see if Jared had left any marks on the side of my head where he had used his elbows on me.

The spot where he hit me was tender to the touch.

Some dancers I knew walked into the bathroom, chattering so loud that it made my head spin. I pulled the coke out of my top. This was Jared's coke, my "prize" for his raping me. Still upset, I offered to share the cocaine with the other girls. They were shocked, as they were well aware that I didn't touch that stuff. But after what had just happened, taking cocaine didn't seem particularly awful; I needed to block out the entire scene, from my acceptance of the offer to the moment on his couch and the sofa. He even had the guts to lock me in!

My thoughts were a mess. Had I really just been raped, or was it just a figment of my imagination? Can a stripper even get raped? Did I deserve this for being so stupid? So many difficult questions raced around my mind, and the only thing that helped quiet my thoughts was drugs. The next day and even the day after, it felt like his smell was still on me, even if I bathed six times a day. It made me nauseous. I hated myself for what I had let happen.

I hated not just that man, but all men. Someone needed to pay.

The next night at work, I began to get constant phone calls in the locker room. They were all from Jared. He would even change his name when I ignored him so that I would answer the phone.

Jared was a persistent man. He called me for one whole year straight because I had given him my home phone number before at the club the night I took his call. I demanded that he stop, but the calls just kept coming. I even called the police, but they said they couldn't do anything about him calling. After I was informed about a new invention called caller ID, I called the phone company, ordered it, and blocked his number as well. It didn't help the mess I felt in my head.

But when the block took effect, I was relieved, believing that I was free of his persistent calls. But it only took Jared a week to figure out how I was avoiding him, and then he started it all over again. Jared began to call with different numbers, but the Caller ID showed that it was a number I didn't know or recognize, so I would not answer the phone. I was so annoyed at his audacity. All I could think was, *how dare this jerk rape me and still have the nerve to stalk me?* He called my home and the locker room at work for me.

I never reported the rape to the authorities or even to the club where I worked, because I assumed that no one would believe that a stripper turned down sex, especially for the money. I felt that my hands and tongue were tied. I didn't even know if I was permitted to feel that way.

After a year, the phone calls stopped, but I began to be followed home by a van. It would stop at the front of my apartment when I returned from the club and stay there until the following day. Was there no stopping this man?

One afternoon at the club, I received a package. It was one of the freaking shoes that I had left at Jared's house in my bid to get out undetected. I couldn't understand why he had done that. He already got what he wanted, so why wouldn't he leave me alone?

There were some days I would see Jared's van parked outside the club, presumably waiting for me. Instead of going home alone, I would ask friends to spend the night with me. Their presence made me feel safe, as I knew he wouldn't try to do anything when there were lots of people around. Eventually, Jared stopped following me in his van, but he showed up at the club where I worked instead.

Unbelievable! My initial reaction was fear. It was the same way I had felt that night at his house; I thought I might pee on myself as I suddenly couldn't feel my legs anymore.

But this was *my* space. This was my place, and I ran what I did in this club. I had many people backing me. The thought of having some of the guys at the club beat Jared up scared me a little. What if Jared started to haunt my life in crazier ways?

But I needed some way to show Jared that I wasn't alone. The club owner never let anyone mess with us, so it wasn't so bad telling him all that transpired. After I told my boss what was going on, he and his bouncers took Jared outside and kicked his butt delivering a beating that he wouldn't forget. This moment came to an end.

"Don't you ever call for me, come for me, or accidental cross my path. I will end you." I meant it. I was done being scared and bothered.

In an instant, Jared was no longer a problem for me. But the same couldn't be said about the coke. I wished getting rid of that problem would be as easy as getting rid of Jared. I later learned that this specific problem wasn't going anywhere anytime soon.

12

Missing All the Turns

I was hooked on cocaine. It helped me cope with all the stress in my life. Even though I knew it was wrong, it felt so right.

Every time I did cocaine, I fell deeper into the pit. But giving up the habit is not as easy as just putting it away and never looking at it again.

So, I continued doing cocaine. Quitting seemed like so much work!

So, I took the "easier" route and continued dancing in spite of these clear signs to stop.

Often men would confuse dancers for prostitutes; I never liked that. But it happened so many times that eventually I came to terms with this too.

I decided that if guys wanted to get screwed, well, I was going to screw them but not the way they wanted! Sometimes men would proposition me outright for sex. Whenever one of them made it clear he was propositioning me for sex, I would reply that for $300, yes, I would screw him. Not in those exact words, of course; I wasn't a stupid girl. If the man agreed, I would send him into one of the private rooms after collecting my money. Then I would send my manager in after him. My manager would tell this man that if he didn't leave right away, he would go directly to jail. I never once had any intentions of having sex with these bastards. These men never argued, but just left. My manager would get a hundred dollars, and I would keep the other two hundred. The men had been screwed – not like they wanted – but how I thought they should be. This is exactly what they deserved for mistaking me for a prostitute, as that rapist Jared had done. I was never a prostitute and I'd be dammed if I would allow someone to mistake me for one.

I was making money again. It didn't matter how many guys I "screwed" or how many dances I was performing on any given night, it all ended up going to clubbing and cocaine. Hundreds and hundreds of dollars going right up my Hoover, and I didn't stop to think about what I was doing. Everything I was doing, from misleading customers to using drugs, was morally wrong.

The old Tyra was gone, and in her place was an angry animal ready to strike out at anyone who dared to get too close.

One night in the club, there was another raid. An officer pointed at me and told me to go sit by the door. I had just arrived and hadn't done any dancing. Why was I being arrested again? What was going on?

My boss had known me to be a clean dancer, and after my last arrest a year before, I knew better than to dance too close to customers. So why was I being singled out? The officer who arrested me would not say. After I posted bond, I found out that it was for solicitation of prostitution. There had to be a mistake. Yes, we ran scams, but only on jerks that solicited me.

I had never or have ever solicited anyone for sex.

At that point in my life, I felt sex was to be given away for free, and boy, did I give it away. I could not believe this was happening. There was no way I was guilty. I was so confused. When I got to court the next week, the district attorney read the report, and I finally knew what had happened. One week before the raid, a girl named Macy (Aka Hollywood) solicited an off-duty officer. They had her name, address and phone number, but because we were both black that night, they took me. I was guilty of being black, and cute at the wrong time.

When I eventually saw pictures of Hollywood, I couldn't believe that anyone could confuse us. Yes, we both had grey eyes. Yes, we both had long hair, and yes, we were both black. But I was prettier, and Hollywood looked a lot more ghetto.

All I needed to do was show that I was in Austin with friends on the night Hollywood had allegedly solicited the undercover officer. It was not easy; I had to track down a few people by phone and get them to confirm the details, but eventually I gathered enough evidence and witnesses to leave no doubt that the police had arrested the wrong girl.

For weeks after that, the police knew they had made a mistake. This arrest mix-up was frustrating like nothing else. Why was I held for something I didn't even do?! Again, that other part of my brain started to speak up to me. It told me to focus on what an awful mess my current employment had landed me in. It told me to take this as a warning sign and change tracks.

I knew I needed a change in employment, but I still refused to change. Sometimes, even now I think of how my life would have had turned out if I had just pulled the brakes and turned to God for guidance.

Eventually, the charge of prostitution was dismissed, but the arrest remained on my record. This stupid mix up ended up costing me a lot more than just a bruise to my already bruised ego.

For eleven years after that, I could not get a job because prostitution was on my criminal record. All arrests show up on your background checks, even if they are dismissed. Eventually, I was able to get that arrest expunged, but for a long time the prostitution label closed doors for me. Every time I would try to steer myself on a different career route, the prostitution label would follow me and ruin my chances. Just as the scarlet letter started to become a permanent part of her identity, I was beginning to think that my past sins would mark me for the rest of my life.

By the way, I later learned that Hollywood – the girl responsible for this wrongful arrest – ended up getting twenty-five years for armed robbery. There is no justice like justice, and eventually even Hollywood had to pay heavily for her sins, but what good did that do to me? As far as I was concerned, the damage had already been done.

I am not trying to downplay my choices or justify them; I knew that the path I was on was less than noble; dancing my nights away in front of random men was hardly something a person aspired to be doing. But if there is one consolation in all of this it is this: I was honest with myself.

I was honest with myself that I needed money. I was honest with myself that other than stripping, no other job would put that much money on the table. I was honest with myself that I had no other talents, skills, or even the education that's required to hold a respectable career other than stripping. I was honest with myself that I knew God was there for me, but I just did not want to do the hard work of turning my metaphorical car in His direction.

But what good is honesty when it won't save you from trouble?

13

Living is Hard When You are Dead

You don't necessarily have to die to be dead; you could be living and still dead. Things in my life continued moving in a downward spiral. Whatever money I was making I immediately spent on buying drugs. Each time I needed a little more than the last time to get high, which meant buying more drugs and spending an increasing amount of money.

So, I kept spending money on drugs, kept on doing them, kept on going to parties. My social life was still not going anywhere though. I met a few interesting men and even dated them for a while, but my partying always got in the way.

My heart was broken every time a relationship ended, and nothing could fill the emptiness inside. After the last guy I had dated left town, I decided I could not stand my life anymore – that is, until he decided to come back. As it turned out, he came back to town just to break up with me. Can you imagine my luck?

And what did I do? Did I cry? A little. To ease the pain, I did the one thing I knew best: took cocaine to rush through my days and Xanax to put myself to sleep at night.

The pain and emptiness would not go away, and I didn't want to live anymore. I was dying inside. My life had become a joke; these where not the plans I had for my life. I used to have dreams and plans; drugs and heartbreak were never part of those plans. I was now 24 and I had nothing. Something had to give!

I had already been up for a couple of days on a coke bender, so I was not thinking clearly. That was when he broke up with me. I got a twelve-pack of Budweiser and a whole bunch of pills – 50 to be exact. I filled my bathtub with water and got in. I drank every beer and took every single one of the pills. I began to cry.

"God," I thought to myself. "I know my life has been a bunch of crap and it's a big joke, but I can't do this anymore. I hurt all the time, and I have no reason to live." I felt my consciousness leaving, and I managed to mumble out some final words. "If you can't give me a reason to live and if there is no reason for me to live, please … just … let … me … die." I remember asking forgiveness for everything I had been doing and for turning my back on him.

The people that I was partying with me found me in the tub after a couple of hours. I was unconscious. It is always a bad situation when someone OD's; often the person will get left behind in a trash can or dumpster somewhere. Since I was already at my place, my friends decided to wait it out. They wanted to see if I would pull through. Angel called poison control, and they told her to get me to throw up and to call an ambulance. They also told her that I would need to go to the hospital no matter what because the number of pills I had taken would cause inevitable liver damage.

There were too many drugs around for them to call an ambulance though, so they decided to make me throw up and hope for the best. When I finally woke up, I walked into my living room naked and told them to keep it down, that I was trying to sleep. From what I understand, I was unconscious for about forty-eight hours before making that announcement.

Everyone in my apartment fell silent for a moment and then began to cheer. I guess no one really wanted to leave me to die alone.

Things were slow after my unsuccessful attempt at killing myself. A week later I didn't feel much better about my life. I still felt like there was no reason for me to live. I noticed that I was getting really sick all the time, but I was also super hungry.

This was particularly strange because usually when you use cocaine, you don't get hungry.

What was up with that? I backtracked a little and noticed that I hadn't had my period. Could I be pregnant? I know a lot of women in my shoes probably think that getting knocked up is the last thing they would want to deal with, but the very idea of having a baby excited me.

I took a pregnancy test, but it turned out negative. I was back where I started: down in the dumps. Now I was even more depressed; at least a baby would have given me a reason to live.

I realized that staying at home all dull and gloomy wouldn't do me any favors. So, I returned to work. I needed to keep busy and I needed to earn some money.

One night after work, a co-worker wanted me to come hang out with one of their friends, a guy, of course. His name was Trent, and little did I know how important a part of my life he would play over the following months.

Trent had a beautiful home in La Porte. He seemed to be doing very well for himself, but he had a pretty big cocaine problem ... even bigger than mine. Trent's problem had been there for a while, and I didn't know it. I was so smitten by Trent's big home that his cocaine problem was the last thing on my mind. After all, I had the same problem; what right did I have to judge?

I started hanging out with Trent a lot. It was only a matter of time until things began to get physical. Trent and I kept seeing each other and grew closer even though both our lives were a mess. During the four months we were together, Trent lost his home and truck and destroyed his credit. I lost my apartment and car; we were homeless. We had both made money, but we lost everything anyway.

I did notice one strange problem though; whenever I would try to do any cocaine, I would get sick and immediately throw up. I had also put on weight.

Could I be pregnant? I did not want to get my hopes up like last time. I decided to go to the Crisis Pregnancy Center near Pasadena and get myself tested.

The test showed that I had been pregnant for a couple of months. I couldn't believe it! Did this mean that when I tried to kill myself a couple of months back, I was already pregnant? But why did the test show negative then? My mind was a blur, partly from confusion but also from excitement.

The people at the Crisis Pregnancy Center were very nice. They gave me several informative pamphlets and advice on how to earn things I needed for the baby, like a bassinet.

There was no question that Trent was the father. He himself had taken me to the crisis center, but he wasn't at all happy that I was pregnant. Did that matter to me? Not in the least! I was pregnant, I was finally going to have a baby of my own. At this point in my life, this was the most important thing that had ever happened. Whenever I brought up my pregnancy, he would get quiet and somewhat frustrated. While that was annoying, I thought I could just ignore and avoid it by not bringing up my pregnancy – until he demanded that I get an abortion.

Trent had his reasons. He was divorced, and he already had one child that he didn't see because of his drug addiction. He was way behind on child support, and he had no desire to deal with another child when he couldn't even be bothered with the one he already had.

But I believed that the baby was a gift, the gift of a new start. God had given me a reason to live. More than anything, I wanted this child, and I wanted to be a good mother. I was hooked on cocaine, but it was making me sick because I was pregnant. I knew I would have to do something drastic, something I didn't want to do, but something I knew I had to do for the sake of this child. I had to call my mother!

When I called my mother, she was excited to hear that I was happy. I asked if I could come home, and she said, "Sure." She told me not to worry about getting a job for a least two months after I had the baby. She was very supportive. I wish I could say that all of my problems were solved when I turned to my mother, but nothing in life is that simple. I knew a cocaine problem was bad; what I didn't know was that getting over a cocaine problem would be even worse. By going home, I managed to isolate myself from everything and everyone associated with drugs, but that demon named cocaine still called to me.

In my dreams and even when I was awake, I would smell it. This is typical for someone trying to get free of drugs. Sometimes it's not because they don't want to quit; mentally they can't. The drug dreams are so vivid, and nearly everyone who comes off drugs has them. Every day for the rest of my pregnancy I craved the stuff. It was complete, unadulterated torment. It was ok, though, because I knew that my baby and I were safe, wanted, and loved at my mother's house.

I was really worried about the damage that I may already have done to my baby, so I was very open and honest with the doctors about my drug use and my suicide attempt. They ran multiple tests and found that my baby was going to be healthy, but with any speed drugs you run the risk of having a hyperactive child. I stayed clean throughout my pregnancy and looked forward to the time after my son's birth when I could return to drugs. They called to me and I wanted to answer.

14

The Baby Blues

On the 22nd of November, 1997, when I was 24, the Lord gave me the most beautiful baby the world had ever seen. At that moment in my life, my son was a sign that God had been with me through all of my pain and struggles. He seemed so happy, smiling at the world in the small crib he was put in. When I mentioned it, the nurse said it was just gas, but it felt like an angel was smiling at me. And I decided to take it that way; I gave birth to an angel.

As happy as I was to have him, I was still drawn to the life I had at the club. Two weeks after the birth of my child, I was back at the point where I started, dancing away at the spot I knew best. My excuse was that I had to make money to cater to my baby's needs. I told my mother this every time she asked me, so much that I began to believe it myself. But dancing was just a means to get close to drugs again. My mother found out about this and was displeased, so she worked out a deal with my aunt in Houston to keep the baby while I worked. Despite her disappointment, my mother tried not to judge me. She would have kept my child herself had she not had to work full time to take care of her children, who were still dependent on her.

My son and I were lucky to have an aunt as excellent and patient as mine, as she was very good to us. He lived in her home with her, and I would stop in once a week to bring her a couple of hundred dollars or so to support her. I really missed my baby and thought about him all the time, but I did not want to give up my lifestyle. Maybe it was because of the freedom that it came with. I continued to dance and live with whomever I wanted, as I didn't have any place to live. My life was still in shambles and rearranging it seemed so impossible. I didn't even have proof of any form of education for a sustainable means of livelihood, and any other jobs I was qualified for would not even pay for a place to live. I knew I wanted my son back. I wanted to raise him and prove that I could be a good mother. The best mother. But that wasn't happening anytime soon, seeing as how I lacked parenting skills.

To create a better life for my baby, I took a job as a waitress at another strip club. This was very different from dancing, even if it was in the same environment. It was still a step up, a little more respectable and looked better on a resume. But that still wasn't enough to stop me from doing drugs. I had plans to quit but being in that space intoxicated me more than I was ready to admit. The lights and the attention drew me in like a moth to a flame.

When my son was three months old, I decided to get him from my aunt. I needed him around me to fill up a void that was widening further with each day. He was innocent and perfect, a mix I needed in my mundane and slow life. Every feeling he had toward me was transparent and honest. It was an expression of simplicity in my complicated existence, and I just couldn't bear the distance between the two of us any longer. I put my foot down and brought my angel back to where he belonged, in my arms, regardless of how frail they were. I had found a sitter who would keep him for about two dollars and fifty cents an hour. Since I had known this girl since she got out of rehab a little more than a year ago, trusting her felt as natural as breathing. Besides, I didn't have any other options. It was either that sitter or me.

I went to work on one particular evening and was having a pretty good night when the manager told me I had a phone call in the office. I couldn't imagine who would be calling me at my job, unless it was someone who had no idea of the nature of my career.

"This is Tyra," I said calmly.

"Ms. Tyra, this is Child Protective Services," the voice at the other end of the receiver said, and I felt my heart stop abruptly. "We have your son in our custody. Is there anyone you can make a call to so that we can release him?"

It felt like someone had tipped my world over. In that split second, every terrible scenario ran through my mind.

"What is this about?" I questioned, my mind entering panic mode. "Why do you have my son?"

"We need you to come to 6300 Chimney Rock," the voice responded. "Will you be able to get here?"

I no longer had a car, but I found someone to take me. We drove from Galveston to Houston in only 45 minutes, but it still managed to feel like an eternity. I was terrified of what might have happened, praying hard that he was not hurt.

I ran into the CPS building without waiting for the person who drove me. My mother and little sister were already there with my son. Cameron, my son, appeared fine, but the glares from my mother and sister were more than enough to tell me that something serious had happened. When I asked what was going on, the attendant said that the police had only just brought in the baby, and the report wasn't in yet. He added that my son could not be released to me, and that if I went anywhere near him, he could also be taken from my mother.

I still didn't have a clue as to what was going on or what I could possibly have done. I looked around, confused, feeling the beginnings of my world crashing all over again. After meeting with the CPS caseworker, I realized that my friend from rehab was far from ready for real-world responsibilities. She had taken my son to a bar, told some strangers to watch him, and never returned. The strangers eventually called the police. I was so upset hearing that and I spewed out every curse word I could think of against Rachael, the sitter. But I failed to acknowledge my own role in this situation because I could not see where I had been wrong at the time.

At first, the CPS worker doubted my version of events because of my criminal record. My arrests for public lewdness and prostitution caused the CPS worker to judge me very harshly, expecting no different behavior from someone of that character. I tried to explain that the prostitution case was dropped because I was innocent, but it hadn't mattered. I resorted to pleading rather than logic and rationality, but it felt like everyone was against me, including my mother. Cameron was taken from me, and I wanted to fight that decision with everything in me. I didn't see any fault in myself.

That's another thing about drugs – they warp your perception about the people and situations around you, making you believe that no one is looking over you. It made me think everyone was out to get me, even when they were looking out for my son. I was wrong, but I could only see the good I played in the situation.

I still could not see how many of my choices were affecting my future. My son had been taken from me, and I could not see my part in the whole thing. Depression set in again. This time, I would make Galveston Bay my graveyard. I filled myself with pills and alcohol and walked out into the ocean, talking to God the entire time. I don't remember what I said to Him the day I did it, but He must have been listening because a man pulled me back to shore and wouldn't leave me until I had gotten home safely. The Lord spared my life a second time when I didn't deserve it.

I grieved intensely for my son, but I just could not get it right. I needed my pain to end, or it was going to end me instead. I barely had a place to live, and my grief over the situation was becoming more than I could handle. I had lost my son, and now I couldn't even kill myself without someone suddenly jumping in to rescue me. Why couldn't I just die?

I needed an intervention. Suddenly, it came in all shades of grey and black. I noticed I was feeling unwell and needed medical attention, and it turned out to be another pregnancy. How could this happen again?

I was thrilled with my first child because it was what I needed; what I had searched for. But this time, I was not sure what to do. I'd lost my first child and just gotten locked out of my friend's apartment, where I was squatting for not paying the rent because we had spent all the money on drugs. My life was in crisis mode, and another child did not seem like the answer. My first baby was only six months old, and now I was having another one. I was overwhelmed.

There was only one solution. I had to get rid of it.

I had to come up with some money and I had to do it quickly. I decided to call John.

I met John at the club where he hung out a couple of times. He was a good guy, but he had two obsessions: bodybuilding and his collection of illegal guns! He was very well off too. Despite all the money and opportunities, John stayed away from drugs. I was pretty jealous of that, as I had tried unsuccessfully to be that person.

One thing I liked about John was that he never judged me. He was always trying to help me by giving me a place to stay or advice about jobs. John liked the idea of my son being around, but I was not ready for someone who didn't do drugs and worked during the daylight hours. It would be an alarming contrast and might end up demanding more from me than I could give.

When I discovered I was pregnant, I asked him for advice. His answer to my problem was marriage, with a smile and a gleam in his eyes. But I didn't want to get married, and I also knew that there was no way John could have possibly been the one responsible for my pregnancy.

I couldn't lie to him, not with the amount of affection I could see in his eyes. We, strippers, have two other cardinal rules: "Never screw over good people" and "Only play players." John was not a player, and I wasn't going to pretend that I loved him when he deserved better than that.

He was a good guy, but who wants a good guy when you can have a whole lot of crappy men? That is one of the main issues with wounded women, and that was certainly what I was. I was so busy trying to get love from men who couldn't or wouldn't love me in return that I hadn't made time for a man who truly did love me. When a good man wants a wounded woman, she usually runs off to another loser. Being married and having another child was not in any of my plans. John was utterly against me having an abortion, but it was the only option I had left. I couldn't even go near my son. I felt so lonely.

A couple of weeks later, after having no more money for a room at Motel 6, I found myself going to John again. I knew he would at least give me some shelter, so I hitched a ride to his neighborhood. I was surprised when Tasha, a girl from the strip club, answered the door. It turned out that Tasha had been helping John to get over me. John had moved on.

Tasha made it clear that no other woman would be staying in John's home while she was there. That was fair. I had my chance earlier and let it pass me by. It was my loss, a huge one. That night I wandered the streets because I had nowhere to go. Nowhere to sleep, nowhere to go, no one to want me.

The next day, I called someone I regarded as an abusive loser. I usually wouldn't seek help from a man like this, but I was desperate. To my surprise and relief, this man was willing to help.

"Just find a place and see how much it is," he said without a second thought. "I will give you the money."

I got a room at Motel 6 in Webster. I knew it would take a couple of weeks before he got paid again, so I hitched a ride to Galveston for the next couple of weeks to keep my hotel room.

Finally, he called to give me some money, and I gave him an estimated amount I thought would be enough for my bills.

At least I had a roof over my head for now.

15

Wichita Falls

"Loving Christian Maternity Home. This is Barbara." The voice was warm yet still sounded mechanic, like she had lost every emotion attached to those words, having to say them repeatedly.

"Is this the doctor's office?" I asked as I looked down at the fat yellow book I was holding.

"No, this is a maternity home." Her voice had lost the mechanic pull to it and was now laced with emotion. I could sense that she was a delightful person.

"Hmm." I thought I had it right.

"May I ask what you are looking for?" Barbara asked politely.

"Well, I thought I was calling an abortion clinic," I said hastily, still staring at the book.

The voice on the other end of the line was so calming. Barbara didn't even sound judgmental like every other person might have.

"Ma'am, I not trying to be nosey, but is it for you?" She questioned.

"Yes, ma'am." I found no reason not to be truthful. She didn't even know me.

She kept quiet for a few seconds before saying, "Have you considered any other option, like adoption? There are a lot of families who would love to have a child."

"Ma'am, I don't even have a place to live. And even if I was to carry a child for nine months, I don't know if I could just give it away."

"Well," she started carefully. "Here at Loving Christian, it is always the mother's choice whether or not she wants to keep her baby."

"Really?"

"Really." She sounded so reassuring.

For some reason, I trusted her and her coaxing inquisitiveness. I felt like I could tell her everything without fear of being criticized or judged.

I told her a little more about me, and she told me about the home they operated and that they even had a bed open at the moment. I stopped my thoughts short when she told me they were located in Wichita Falls, Texas. Even if I were interested, how in the world would I get there? Wichita Falls was nine hours away.

After I hung up with Barbara, I realized that in the yellow pages, I had looked through the "abortion alternatives" section and not the area for abortion. I gave the idea of adoption a little more thought, considering it a good enough option. However, there was still the issue of distance. How would I get to Loving Christian Maternity Home? I thought about the possibility of a similar place closer to Houston, so I got a ride to the Crisis Pregnancy Center in Pasadena and talked to a counselor. This way, I thought, I would have a place to live and not be forced to use drugs anymore.

On reaching there, the maternity home needed proof that I was pregnant, and the Crisis Pregnancy Center gave me a letter of confirmation. Peggy, the counselor at the Crisis Pregnancy Center, was accommodating. There was compassion in her eyes as I explained my situation.

There was a little hitch to my newfound plan, however. All the maternity homes in our area only accepted teenagers or mothers who would place their babies up for adoption. While I needed a clean place to stay, I wanted to have the choice to keep my baby. Peggy, the counselor, convinced me to call my mother and discuss it with her.

My mother was happy to hear from me and to know I was okay. She assured me that I could come to visit my firstborn and that her intention was never to keep Cameron from me. She also told me that CPS had finally made a decision about my case. If I took parenting classes, I could have my son back. That was great news, but I knew that I still wasn't ready to take care of Cameron. Not now, with the latest development.

After several more telephone calls, Peggy decided she would drive me the nine hours to Wichita Falls. I was stunned at her generosity, strong faith, and the commitment that inspired her to drive nine hours for a drug addict she didn't know. At that point, Peggy's presence in my life was another sign that God's hand was always at work.

Throughout the trip, I imagined how my life would turn out differently. I thought about how I could make my mother proud, get my son back and go to college. Those were the things I had always wanted. I desired that everything return to the usual and ordinary state, where my son would be happy, and my unborn child would have the best of lives even if there were high odds that I wouldn't be in it. I thought it perfect, as I would be forced to stay away from drugs, and my life would have to change for the better.

Norma, the housemother, was there to greet us when we arrived. She had a sweet, calming disposition, but I doubted her countenance would remain the same if she learned who I really was and how badly I had messed up my life. Although I didn't mind people knowing I had been a dancer, I thought it best to keep my drug history to myself. It was hard to be completely open, even with these people. I had learned about individuals and their distinct personalities a little too early in life that their outward disposition didn't affect my stance.

The house looked peaceful, like an envelope of amassed love and contentment. It was a vast place, with enough space to have a pool built on the roof. The room I was given was big and decorated in a yellow flower pattern, with a joint bathroom to be shared with the girl next door. Maybe I could have a fresh start. It was so calm here that I felt like I could be a new person.

There was no comparing what I had in Wichita Falls with my old place. It was warm and welcoming here, holding no trace of the loneliness and frailty I felt back home. In *The Scarlet Letter*, Hester wonders at one point if there existed a place totally different from Massachusetts Bay Colony where she could live without being judged harshly and severely.

For me, that place was Wichita Falls.

Four pregnant girls stayed together in the house. First, there was Candy, the fourteen-year-old who cried rape when her parents found out the guy who got her pregnant was black. Candy later felt wrong about alleging that the black guy had raped her, as she knew it wasn't right. She just didn't want to lose her innocence in front of her parents. I didn't judge her. I had made my own fair share of mistakes too.

Then there was the 17-year-old Jenny, who had gotten pregnant by a black boy she was in love with. Her parents put her in the maternity home, hoping she would choose to place the child up for adoption. Her parents were humiliated and angry, as they had always been one to criticize teenagers who got pregnant. However, Jenny remained strong-willed, even though her father refused to talk to her.

The last woman in the house was Erika. Erika was the oldest amongst us. She was twenty-eight, with striking features and long red hair. Erika was on probation for stealing sunglasses from a mall. Her boyfriend accompanied her in the acts, stealing to support their crack habit. They eventually got caught and had to deal with the travails of drug withdrawal.

These three girls and I became like sisters, creating a bond that transcended that of mere friends. We all had chores in the house, and although I was not too fond of chores, I did mine well. Norma and I became incredibly close. She treated me like a daughter, always around when I needed someone to talk to. It was the first time that I felt like someone's favorite. That woman felt a special love for me and didn't hesitate to show it. Growing up, I was never the favorite, and although I felt special being chosen to work at Ms. Rachel's house, I knew I was never very dear to her. Being Norma's favorite made me feel important, like I mattered despite everything I was. I thought that maybe, just maybe, if I mattered to her, then I mattered to God. I had faith when I was younger and I had genuinely thought that I mattered to Him. Later, after all I had been through and everything I had done, I lost that belief. I thought there was no way He could love or want me in His kingdom, and that nothing unclean could ever stand before him. Norma was helping me rebuild that faith and confidence.

Life wasn't always perfect in the house. After about two weeks, I started to go through withdrawals because I had stopped using cocaine. I would shiver and endure pounding headaches in silence. Because I didn't want anyone to know I had used it in the first place, telling anyone about the physical and mental torture of narcotics withdrawal was impossible. It was terrible, having to groan, curled up on the bathroom floor in the middle of the night. It would have helped to be able to talk about it. I just wanted someone to hold me, so I would wrap my arms around the baby inside me and let her know I loved her and wanted her to be okay. I wanted her to feel untouched by her mother's travails and I promised that she would never have to see me like that when she arrived. I knew she was a girl because I had just gone to the doctor for an ultrasound, and he confirmed that she was an active and healthy little girl. In addition to suffering from the withdrawals, I was scared about having another baby without a way to support them.

Months went by, and I began to miss my son. I was hurting from it like it was a novel feeling. I wanted him with me. As the baby grew inside me and moved around, I had flashes of the time I was pregnant with Cameron. It was, perhaps, a result of how lonely I felt without him. I shared my sadness with Norma, and she offered to let my son come live in the home with us. I was overjoyed. I had not seen him in six months, and he was turning a year old soon. His new sister would arrive just a month after his birthday, and I wanted us all to be together.

As I waited for arrangements for Cameron to come live with me, I applied to the housing assistance program through the city. A month later, I was also approved for childcare assistance, so I would have somewhere to put Cameron when he came. At last, my life was finally starting to come together. God was in my life, but Satan wouldn't make it easy for Him or me.

I spent a lot of time around Erika, the shoplifter with the crack habit. We confided in each other many times, but she couldn't wait to get back to smoking; that was all she talked about. Unlike herself, I was focused on staying clean. I was already battling drug dreams and had struggled through the painful withdrawals. Luckily for me, cocaine withdrawals don't kill a person. The physical aches and illness weren't fun, but the mental torment was the worst part. Cocaine affects the brain, and I had to battle against Erika's praise for drugs and my strong desire to return to it. I came here to change my life, to get a fresh start for my children and me. But all Erika talked about was crack. Crack, crack, and more crack.

She wasn't helping!

The first eighteen months are critical to overcoming any cocaine addiction. If you are lucky, eighteen months is enough for one's brain to return to normal. But some people take longer, while others never get over it. Cocaine, like heroin, is bad juju.

My mom drove my son up to Wichita Falls one month before I had my little girl. I looked my mother straight in the eye, my happiness radiating everywhere. I was glad I saw Cameron while I was drug-free. It meant a lot to me that I was finally doing something right. However, I noticed that Cameron wasn't very active. Although I could sense that he was as excited as I was, he wasn't moving around as much as other small children tended to do. I didn't give much thought to it at the end of the day, because all that mattered at the time was that I had a beautiful son and another exceptional child on the way. I was happy. The only thing left was how I was going to provide for their needs.

One month later, in December, I had Cindy. She was so beautiful at 7 pounds 11 ounces. It was a tough delivery, and in the end, we both caught a fever and had to stay in the hospital for several more days. Norma was nice enough to stay in the hospital with me, but I was sad to be having a baby with no family around. Although Norma was like family, I still felt alone. It was my second time having a baby without a father, which was always lonely.

After I had Cindy, I returned to the maternity home for a couple more weeks while my body recuperated from the difficult delivery. In January, when I was healthy again, I moved my children and myself into our new apartment in Wichita Falls. Fortunately, things seemed to be going my way, and it continued like that – for about six months.

I enjoyed living in Wichita Falls. During August, the town gets pumped up because the Dallas Cowboys have their training camp there, and everyone hopes to see one of the players. While the Cowboys were in town that year, I worked at a new seafood restaurant. It was a refreshing career change, and I had a lot of fun doing it. I couldn't have asked for more, but surprisingly, it came. That was where I had my very own Cowboy sighting.

Unexpectedly, one of the top guys from the Cowboys, along with his son, came to the restaurant where I worked and invited me to hang out with them at the local bar. I agreed to go with them, and I got drunk on their tab. Not surprisingly, by the end of the night, a pretty dark-skinned girl was dancing at the bar. I couldn't seem to help it as they all cheered me on. You know I love attention!

That wasn't the only run-in I had with a Cowboy. I also got to wait on Troy Aikman and his beautiful blonde fiancée. They were so polite throughout their meal, the quarterback informing the manager on the way out that he'd received some of the best services he'd had in a long time. He even gave me a 30% tip. Aikman was a lovely guy, and people like him made Wichita seem like such a great place.

I was doing well, paying my bills on time and staying clean. For some reason, I suddenly decided to start hanging out again with Erika, the crack addict from the maternity home. We were both young mothers without many girlfriends, and I didn't think hanging out with her would weaken my resolve to stay clean. How wrong could I have been! Before long, I was back to cocaine; it was like I hadn't left.

After about four months of partaking it, something strange happened. I heard my spirit telling me that it was time to make a choice. There was a voice inside me telling me that this lifestyle had to end. The options were to continue to do drugs or choose God. I wasn't sure what to think, because the whole thing was so surreal. Was God really reaching out to me? Or was my lack of sleep making me crazy?

After a lot of thought, I finally became sure that this had to be God telling me that it was time to get it together. So, I made my choice. I chose to live my life to its full potential rather than die on the streets. I decided to be an example to my children. I chose to have food in my refrigerator and pay my electricity bills on time. I chose not to have men running in and out of my home for fear of getting pregnant for the third time. I decided to call my mother and tell her everything I had done. It was one hell of a period, but I was determined, and there was no backing down.

For the first time, I was completely honest with my mother about the cocaine. I was really and truly ready to be done with it all. My mom said she could tell something had been happening when I didn't come home for Christmas. She admitted that I had been on her heart, but she just never thought it would turn out to be drugs. Her voice sounded disappointed, scaring me at the same time. I wanted my mother to forgive me, just like Hester wanted Dimmesdale to forgive her. When he found the truth about Chillingworth's reality, he felt betrayed by Hester. Still, he found it in his heart to forgive her and leave justice to God.

My mother did something similar too. She forgave me, but unlike Dimmesdale, my mother was no hypocrite. In this time of need and desperation, she did not abandon me. She got in touch with people at the church she attended, and they made arrangements for me to return home with Cameron and Cindy. This was it. I left everything I owned at that point in Wichita Falls and decided to make a clean break.

Things are always easier said than done. I had decided that there was no room for drugs in my life, but the temptation was still there. However, this time, whenever the temptation overcame me, I forced myself to think about what was important: The Lord and my family.

There were some withdrawals, but they were not nearly as bad as before. It was like the Lord just took the craving away.

16

The Call

The problem with using cocaine is that you become identified as a "person who uses cocaine." Almost every person assumes things about people who used to be hooked on cocaine, and all kinds of red flags go up. Most employers refuse to give former cocaine users the benefit of the doubt, which became a big problem for me during my search for a job. I spent a lot of time job hunting and failed to secure any. None of the jobs that would consider hiring me paid enough for childcare and a roof over my head. And even though my previous lifestyle called out to me, dancing wasn't an option since I had decided to live a clean and righteous life. I had two children now and I needed a way to raise them properly.

When the Lord asked me to choose in 2000, I committed to my choice and knew my life could never be the same. But after being rejected time and again for jobs, I lost the determination to continue the hard life of change. It was difficult enough without considering my futile efforts at landing myself a job. In a state of depression, I decided to have a bottle of beer at my mother's house. I wasn't expecting her to walk in on me at that moment, and the resulting look on her face was heart-wrenching. She forced me to move out of her house within the month. I was stranded, without a clue as to what to do. I didn't have a whole lot of options, so I took a job at McDonald's as a shift manager. They wanted me to work crazy hours, having to arrive very early and leave late. Apart from that, the grease wreaked havoc on my skin, causing a lot of spots and irritation.

I had told myself that I would never take a job in a fast-food restaurant, but I did what I had to do to make life work for myself and my kids. However, I did not last very long there because the hours wore me out, and the work was physically demanding. Never underestimate the duties of fast-food workers – it's a tough job!

One morning, after working the graveyard shift at the new 24-hour McDonald's in Bacliff, I awoke to my two children pouring syrup all over me. Another time while I was asleep, my kids had cut my hair. The intriguing thing was that they were always right next to each other when they were doing something devious, like when they locked me out of the house so they could rummage through the groceries I had in brought earlier. Ironically, I found them adorable, even when they were misbehaving. However, the syrup and the hair cutting showed me that I couldn't keep working at McDonald's. If I didn't put in a resignation letter, there was a high probability that I might end up being bathed with tomato ketchup next.

Life was a struggle, but killing myself was no longer an option now that I had something to live for. My children were the motivation I needed to keep pushing and striving, even when it threatened to rain cats and dogs. The worst part of my being poor was the welfare system. Standing in those queues for so long, having to beg for food, with people treating you like a second-class citizen are experiences I wouldn't wish on the most despicable person. I hated those offices and felt humiliated every time I left. But there wasn't any other option available to me. My children needed to eat, and we needed a place to live. A mother sacrifices for her children, even if she has to offer up her pride every now and again. My kids were worth that sacrifice, and now that I think about it, I'm optimistic I could go through that all over again if it means making them comfortable.

One day my mother allowed me to use her car to go job hunting, so I rode around, putting in applications and keeping my fingers crossed. I decided to sing and pray as I drove around Webster. Turning off the radio so I could speak to the Lord, and He could hear me loud and clear, I began to pray for guidance. As I prayed harder, I felt a rushing wind, and suddenly, a voice that could have only been from heaven said, "GO to School!"

I was so surprised that I had just heard the voice of God, so much that I doubted it for a few seconds. I knew I wanted to go to school, not just to a technical school or beauty school, but to a College. This wasn't just a passing idea. I knew it was God answering my prayer for guidance. The presence in the car was overpowering, and I knew I just had to obey.

Listening immediately, I got off the freeway and headed down to Alvin, Texas because I knew there was a college there. I drove to Alvin Community College, knowing I was on the right path. I had an assurance that I wasn't making a mistake, that this was what I was meant to be doing.

This reminds me of something a preacher once told me. He said, "Do you know how I know the Lord is talking to me? Well, he sounds a lot like me. Do you know what the devil sounds like when he's talking to me? Well, he sounds a lot like me too." Confusing, right?

The day the Lord spoke to me, he sure did sound a lot like me. How could I be confident that it was the Lord guiding me and not just another sudden idea of my own?

Faith!

I had absolute faith that it was the Lord Almighty speaking to me. The assurance came in a mild form, and I felt peace in my heart taking that new leap. Faith is an essential part of following the right path. Knowing and understanding God's strategic plan is vital to your spiritual growth.

In Jeremiah 1:5, God tells Jeremiah, "Before you were in the womb, I knew you and set you apart." If God knew us before we were in the womb and had already set us apart, that means there was a plan set in motion for our lives before our conception. I believe in predestination, and I am conscious that I have often fallen short, but if we repent and we are still alive, there is another strategic plan set in motion for our lives. Our primary responsibility, as humans, is to stay on track, possible by prayer and doing what we know to be right by God. It is not always popular to do the right thing, but it is necessary and will lead you to the destination God has waiting for you. It just tends to take time, but what's destiny without patience?

When I arrived at Alvin Community College, I asked someone, presumably a student, where I could find the administrative office. The people on the campus were so lovely, making the whole task more effortless than I had imagined. I walked down a busy hallway, nervous about whether I really heard God on the entire go-to-school thing. I was hoping for a sign to confirm that this was what God wanted for me, even when the signs were everywhere. Perhaps, my nervousness made it easy to lose sight of them.

I finally made it to the administrative block, where I was told to wait for a counselor. She was a blond woman in her late forties, with beautiful eyes that seemed to wrap themselves around me. In her office, she was playing KSBJ, one of Houston's local Christian radio stations. I took this as the sign I had asked for and felt comfortable as I told her that I thought the Lord was telling me to go to school.

I sincerely told her, "I don't even have any money to afford it, but I just knew I was supposed to come out here."

"Well, have you thought about what degree you would like to get?" She asked, turning down the volume of the radio set.

"Well, I think I would be good at counseling." I never thought I was smart enough for school after being held back twice in elementary school. I wasn't smart and did not know if I had what it took to be successful in school. I had to believe that if the Lord was leading me in this direction, He had to have a plan for my success in it, along with the means to providing for myself and my family.

"Wow, this is definitely God!" she exclaimed. "It just so happens that the mental health department has scholarships for people who desire to become a licensed chemical dependency counselor or an LCDC. These people get their associate's degree in mental health and are licensed as an LCDC. And if you want, they could transfer you to the University of Houston to get your bachelor's degree in psychology or any other behavioral-related field."

I know had asked for a sign, but this was more like a billboard. Was God really going to give me a scholarship to college? I was dumbfounded. My counselor sent me over to speak to Dr. J. Carrier, head of the mental health department.

Dr. Carrier was a well-educated man with red hair and glasses hanging from the bottom of his nose. His impeccable attitude made the interview easy and pleasant. He never made me feel like I was any less of a human because I wasn't educated. I felt like I was on the same plane as him, which made me even more vocal during the interview. He was so approachable!

Dr. Carrier informed me that the scholarships would cover all of my class expenses and the purchase of books. I could not believe how quickly all this was happening, from a simple car ride searching for a job to landing myself an interview at the college!

In all the excitement about the scholarship, a slight concern still sprung up. I barely made it through high school while I was younger, so how was I supposed to make it through college? College was for the big riders. I was in my late twenties with two children, without a place to call my own. Wondering how this was all going to work out, I went ahead and filled out all the paperwork. And just like that, it was official. I was registered for college on a scholarship, with classes commencing in two weeks.

When I got back to my mother's house, she was not happy that I had been gone for so long with her car. She was worried that something had occurred. And with all that had happened to me, I didn't blame her for thinking that way!

I was excited about starting school again. And even though I was tempted to tell my mother about it, I didn't because I wasn't sure how it would work out, that was *if* it worked out.

I put all this aside to focus on more pressing matters. Because the last time I thumbed through the Yellow Pages brought such a positive result, I tried my luck again, looking for available shelters. Many of them required clients to leave the shelter during the day to seek work. That wouldn't work for me because my children could not be without care. Right, there was another obstacle I hadn't even considered. How would I go to school if I didn't have anyone to look after my kids?

Dread crept up my spine at that moment. Did the Lord set me up on all of these aspirations, just to get disappointed? Was it the penalty for my sins? Had he given me free tuition that I wouldn't be able to use? Maybe He didn't tell me to go back to school after all. I must have heard wrong.

What horrible luck! I was so upset at myself for not even thinking about childcare before I registered for the classes. What type of mother was I, thinking about myself first when I was offered the opportunity?

The next day I borrowed my mother's car again, giving her a specific time to expect my return so she wouldn't get all worried again. I drove back to Alvin Community College to unregister for my classes, crying all the way there. During the ride, I repeatedly asked, "Why, Lord?" My faith was wavering. Although I genuinely believed that I had heard from God, I didn't understand why it was so difficult to make this work.

In tears, I checked in to see the counselor I had talked to before, telling her I would have to be a college dropout before I had even started, because I had no means of getting childcare. The woman calmly listened as I explained my difficulties.

"Let's see what we can do," she said, getting off her seat.

She brought me to a different office, where I met another counselor who introduced herself as the childcare facilitator for the college. She told me that they had a certain number of childcare scholarships, but unfortunately, they had allocated all of them already. I was too late.

"Thank you for your help," I said to her as I turned to leave, heartbroken.

"Wait a minute," she called out as I reached the doors. "I have a friend that works for the Texas Work Source. I'm going to call her. Hold on a minute."

My pulse quickened, and I prayed with all the faith I had left that I would get a positive response.

After the childcare facilitator talked on the phone to her friend, she handed me a business card. "I'm not making any promises," she said with pleading eyes. "But my friend might be able to help."

An hour later, I arrived at a big, shiny building where the Texas Work Source was located, hoping to get an appointment while also trying not to get my hopes high. Reaching the reception, I asked to see the woman whose name was on the business card. Minutes later, an attractive woman with brown, shoulder-length hair approached me.

"You must be the young lady from Alvin Community College," she looked so bright and excited. "Tell me how I can help you."

I was stunned that I hadn't needed an appointment to see her. Maybe God was working for me after all!

Nervous about meeting this woman, I decided to be completely honest, not wanting to take any chances. I explained how God delivered me from drugs and then told me to go to school. I also told her how I could get a scholarship but might be forced to drop out before I even started because I couldn't afford childcare for my children. I asked myself suddenly if I had really just told the woman that I had heard God speak to me. I felt sure she would have me escorted out for exhibiting traits of insanity.

The Work Source Regional Superintendent, who was the man in charge, was there that day and overheard every part of my story. He stepped into the conversation and said, "So, God told you to go to school, huh?" He stared me right in the eye, wanting to see if I was being serious or if I was just plain crazy.

"Umm, yes, sir," I replied calmly. In my heart, I knew the Lord had been talking to me in the car a few days ago. I wouldn't back away from that statement, even if the Superintendent thought I was crazy.

"I haven't met many young women like you," the Superintendent said, seemingly impressed. "Because of what you just told us, if you want to go to school, we will pay for your childcare and schooling."

"Well, sir, ACC already said they would pay for my schooling and books." I wasn't expecting such a reaction.

"Ma'am," he started. "I am never in these offices, which means the paperwork I am doing for you today would normally take a couple of months to get to me. In most cases, the person applying would go on a waiting list. But for you, I'll see that the paperwork gets done immediately, so this won't happen. We want to pay for your school, books, and childcare." He concluded with an air of finality.

As the man began doing my paperwork, I kept my mouth shut like the intelligent girl I thought I was at that point. I didn't want to do anything to jinx this miraculous offer, so I had to tread carefully. It was hard to believe that my luck was finally starting to turn around. Two organizations wanted to fund my schooling without me having to give heaven and earth. I couldn't fathom it.

The man gave me a card and said they might also be able to help with gas funds. Then abruptly, he disappeared into thin air. If I hadn't had the papers, contracts, codes of ethics, and many other documents that needed my signature, I might have thought I had imagined him. You have no idea if you think my mind was blown at this point. Just wait!

I looked at the card that the Superintendent had given me. It was for the Texas disability office, the building right around the corner. Apparently, recovering from drugs was considered a form of short-term disability. When I arrived there, I met a lady named Siad. She was a beautiful woman in a wheelchair. I walked in with just the card, but in return, I walked out with another organization that wanted to pay for my schooling and books. For gas, they offered to give me twenty dollars a week, which was more than adequate at the time.

God had organizations fighting to pay for my college. I think that is called confirmation. It felt good to know that I mattered to Him.

Back to School, Back to Life

The Lord made it possible for me to become a college student but doing the actual schoolwork was a different ball game. It didn't help that I had never been a good student and always struggled with studying. After being held back in my first and third grades, you can imagine how anxious and unsure of myself I felt when commencing classes. How on earth would I survive college if I had problems in a class as easy as a third grade?

My kindergarten teacher was tall, blonde, and beautiful, with one of the friendliest smiles I had ever seen. Because of the number of students in my class at the time, I don't remember the teacher ever having sufficient time to talk to me. I vividly remember one time when the teacher walked around the classroom, praising the kindergarteners' drawings. She had stopped by the table next to me, telling the student how beautiful her drawing was. There was a sudden desire to hear my teacher say she liked mine also, so I drew a picture just like the one the girl next to me had drawn. It was the sketch of a girl in a dress with a C-shaped hair colored black. I was sure the drawing would earn praise and a compliment from the teacher, and excitedly, I raised my hands to get her attention.

"Is my picture pretty?" I asked, the display of my white teeth showing how excited I was.

"No," she said. "This is ugly! Can't you do better?" She scrunched her face up and glared at me as she continued walking around the classroom, monitoring the progress of the rest of the class. I was crushed that day, and it ceased to make any difference to me if I studied hard or not.

It is ridiculous that one comment said to me so long ago still had so much power over me. I believed I was not smart enough, good enough, and could not do the work expected of me, so I didn't make any effort. It still wouldn't have been good enough.

And now here I was, about to go to college. The notion felt surreal, even up to the moment I stepped into a lecture theatre for the very first time.

When classes started, there was much anticipation about what it would be like. Were my teachers going to like me? How long was I going to last before I failed as expected? Were there going to be any cute guys? Yes! I wondered about that last bit quite often, as well. I was still me.

When I loved to play volleyball and basketball in junior high school, I was often ineligible to be a part of the team due to my grades. In eighth grade, I realized it was no longer popular to be stupid, and I wanted to fit in with students who seemed to have aims and desired something out of life. It had not been easy, and all I could muster up with my newly cultivated study habits were high C's, but this was better than I had ever done. I constantly asked myself how I would make it through college as I prepared to start my classes at ACC. College was a whole different ball game.

My first day of classes arrived with all of those thoughts and doubts and embedded anticipation. You would not believe the course was about drug use and abuse. God sure has a good sense of humor.

This class was always interesting, as it covered various types of drugs and their effects on the body. With their similar characteristics, sometimes I felt that I had already tried every drug in the book, but apparently, and dare I say, fortunately, that wasn't true. I never realized how many different substances could be abused, not to mention their effects on the body and brain, until taking that class.

My fascination with the subject matter paid off. Maybe it was a result of my history of drug usage, but at the end of the first semester at ACC, I had all A's and B's! Teachers talk about "rigor and relevance." Well, studying drugs as a disease was already relevant to my life. If a student believes that a subject is relevant to herself, she is more likely to remember and retain the facts and concepts than she otherwise would if she had no attachment to it.

If the Lord tells you to do something, he will never set you up for failure. Unlike humans, He is somebody who keeps His word. Just like Abraham believed in God, we need to believe in Him because whatever He promises, He performs. It was just like how God told me to go to college, and that's what I ended up doing!

I won't pretend it was easy, because it took every bit of willpower I had not to give up halfway because of the stress I went through studying. God had worked out so many of the practical details of my education, but it was still up to me to learn, turn in assignments, and at the same time, manage two hyperactive, out-of-control children, all on my own. It took a lot of effort and determination to make God's plan a reality. As glad as I was that I was finally putting my life in order, I still often felt incredibly alone. There was no closure with education, and it ate at me most times.

I started going to church. Living Faith Outreach in Dickenson, Texas, would be my church home for the next eight years. The pastors there, John and Jeana Gilligan, were like second parents to me. They made sure I stayed on the straight and narrow, reiterating that I dared not leave even if the skies got cloudy. I would often get phone calls from different church members to ensure that I was all right and that I didn't need anything. As a result, I made it my mission to be at every service in the year 2000 and would always bring carloads of women from the shelter with me. I am proud to say that I helped many friends from the shelter to give their lives to God, and I was happy doing it. It felt fulfilling, like I was finally doing something that brought closure to me.

I was still schooling at Alvin Community College, but transportation became an issue along the way, so my Pastor's wife, Jeana, offered to drive me to school. While this was an incredible blessing, I knew it wasn't right to let her put herself out so much for me, but I didn't have any other means available, so I prayed about it and hoped God would show me a way to make it work.

Shortly after I put this issue on my prayer list, God took care of it. It is incredible how He can take care of so many things if you just trust him with your concerns. On one of the many drives, the Pastor suddenly informed me that the church was going to buy me a car. I was so stunned at the declaration that I couldn't say anything for a minute.

They were true to their word and bought me a car a few days after.

It wasn't anything new or flashy and it was certainly a fixer-upper. But it didn't matter to me, as I was just so happy to have it. With my need for a car out of the way, job hunting would become more manageable, and I could use all my cash to get a place to live.

While I was glad that I finally had a car, it did not solve all my problems immediately. The search for a job was very discouraging, so much so that I gave up several times along the way. No one was interested in hiring me between my background check and college hours. My past seemed to follow me everywhere I went, like a cancerous growth. As I continued to look for a job with no positive results, I started getting nervous. I wanted to leave the shelter and I couldn't do that without a job.

After a few weeks of a futile search, I began to pray. I was tempted to dance again just to get out of the shelter. Time and again, Satan seductively whispered in my ear that dancing was the only way out of my situation. I prayed desperately to God for help, hoping He wasn't tired of hearing my calls.

I found another way out because I knew I could not go down that road again. God answered, not with a call-back to any of the places I had applied, but in own His beautiful way. It was amazing how the people at church suddenly started to approach me with work that they needed to have done, from house cleaning to fixing things in their homes. I took every opportunity, working twice as hard as I ever had. When it was time to leave their homes, the church members would sometimes bless me with a hundred dollars more than my rendered services required. I was pulling in enough money, along with my financial aid from the school. I would be able to get a place for me and the kids, which was so relieving.

I found a cheap apartment close to school. It was one of the most affordable in the town of Alvin, but I wanted to make sure I could easily walk to school if I ever had car trouble. I worried about not having furniture, but there wasn't any need to, as one day, I surprisingly found that my apartment was full of furniture. I had known the church was coming by, because I had left the door open for some of them who had offered to get me some things. I just hadn't realized that they would be so generous, rendering so much help in my time of need. I will never forget my denim couch. It was the most admirable piece of furniture I had since I stopped dancing. When I sat on that couch, it felt like things weren't so bad, like my life might actually get better. I continued to work hard in my classes, cared for my children, and prayed for a better life for Cameron, Cindy, and myself.

At that point in my life, one of my most significant sources of strength was the women from my church who constantly called and checked up on me. My family at that church was an honest reflection of God at work in the world. They had so much love and selflessness infused in their being that I could see the sacrifice of Christ playing out in them. I am yet to see another church family who invested as much time and effort in me as this one had. Ms. Dylis, the church administrator and principal of the private school, took time out of her busy schedule to disciple me. She prepared Bible study sessions for me and talked with me every week about growing with God and instructed me on how to face the struggles in my life. She also gave parenting advice and tips, knowing I would need them with the bundle I had on my hands. The people at my church knew how much of a mess I was and they didn't care. They prayed for me, watched out for me, and offered support without judgment.

People seem to know when they are being judged, and it drives a wedge between the person being judged and what God wants to do for them. That's why Jesus told us not to judge lest we be judged. We do not want to suffer God's wrath for our actions. Even those who have led a so-called "good life" without accepting Jesus are ultimately lost. Passing judgment on the lost is useless because they are lost and will make no difference. We are called to seek them out and save them, but it is only through the power of God and the blood of Jesus that any can be saved.

After living in that apartment for a year, I made friends in the town of Alvin. Although my church family offered me a great deal of support and comfort, I was still a young woman who needed to hang around with other women of my age group. It was at this period I met April and Mandy, my neighbors.

April and Mandy lived a few doors down from my apartment. Sometimes, we would prepare barbecue together on the weekends, sharing stories as we set up the grill. When we were done eating, they would go to a local bar where they could do karaoke for the night. This seemed like harmless fun until I realized that April and Mandy were both doing Ecstasy.

It glared at me for a while, yet I had been overlooking the signs because I wanted to block out that aspect of my past. I was disappointed but continued to hang out with them for the last month of my lease.

April had introduced me to a guy named Jason, and I really liked him. He seemed to like me too, and I thought maybe I had found a permanent boyfriend, until I found out he had his own demons.

I learned he shot up.

This was more than a turnoff and frightened me, so I immediately broke off our budding relationship. Jason responded by threatening to kill me and my children if I didn't get back together with him. I should have known that anyone introduced to me by April would be that way. I was scared. I recognized this kind of dangerous behavior. Jason was like my father, and I didn't want anyone like that near my children.

When Pastor Jeana found out about the type of people I was hanging out with, she gave me the words I desperately needed. She reminded me of what I had told her about God's message to me, repeating the phrase, "Make a choice."

She was right that I just needed some reminding. I was twenty-five now and hardly a kid anymore. I needed to make better choices.

The church offered me another great source of support during this rough transition: a Bible study group called Esther. After noting signs of my sudden depression, Lynn, a church member who was also a nurse, decided to start the Esther group. The group would meet once a month and have Bible study fellowships. This was an excellent outlet for women who attended, and it was just what I needed. We could talk about anything and everything, and the best part was that there was childcare. Esther group was God's solution to my boredom and loneliness, allowing me to be social with people who would support and encourage my faith and healthy lifestyle.

18

The Turning Point

After my apartment lease was up, I moved back to a shelter. The Bay Area Turning Point was to be my home for the next six months, and I expected it to be a traditional shelter, but I was surprised when I saw it – it was nothing like the others.

The Bay Area Turning Point had to be the best shelter I had ever been in. The location was kept secret so women who lived there would be safe from their abusive spouses. The shelter's sole mission was to provide recovery solutions for survivors of domestic violence and sexual assault. As part of that, the shelter introduced residents to violence-prevention strategies to effect societal change. They had sessions where it was treated with utmost skill and precision. It was the perfect place for me.

Living in a shelter is never easy. While you gain a roof over your head with the daily opportunity to learn new things, you also have to pay attention to the shelter's rules, as flaunting them means you already have another place to live in. Dealing daily with many people you don't know very well takes you on another journey that could either end positively or negatively.

These women and children were hurting, and while I felt for them deeply, I realized that abused women could also be angry and extremely demanding. The strangest thing I encountered in the shelter was that some women would gang up on the others. It wasn't done in the traditional sense, where they got together and physically attacked the other women. I guess they were too mature for that. Instead, they would come together to do rude and hurtful things to other women, and sometimes even their children.

It was troubling to see hurt women strike out at other abused women. It felt like the abused was turning into the abuser, and the prevalent helplessness on both sides further facilitated their acts. However, the Turning Point staff managed these situations well, as they were constantly aware of this behavior and nipped it in the bud whenever possible. I guess the awareness came from the number of years the shelter had been running and the various types of women seeking solace there.

The shelter offered many opportunities for women to grow on their own. We learned about the cycle of abuse and how to recognize abusive behaviors. The shelter also provided many services, including group therapy, transportation, schooling assistance, childcare, legal help, medical service, and other similar services. There I learned to take control of my actions and live up to my responsibilities. It was a steppingstone for me, seeing as I was a mother of two who needed to understand what it truly meant to live up to responsibilities.

All the girls at the shelter loved to have barbecues at Clear Lake Park in the Greater Bay Area of Houston. It was a beautiful park next to the water and an excellent place to get away from daily pressures and forget the events in which the outside world had brought us together. It was a time to let go of all that held us and laugh sincerely under the sunlight, with the cool air from the water serving as a welcoming refreshment. On Saturday, the girls and I went to our usual spot in the park, but this time we decided to bring along some cans of beer. We were all having a good time chatting about our lives when I saw one girl we hadn't invited because she seemed to enjoy getting people in trouble. As soon as I saw her, I knew our decision to have some fun time out there was over. But it was so much more than that.

It was only a matter of time before everyone attending the barbecue would have to find another place to live. We had all signed a contract saying that we would not drink or do drugs while living there, and we had clearly broken that contract.

For the rest of that day, we lived in trepidation. Nothing really happened until the following day when the staff began calling us in for interviews. When interviewed about our outing, each of the other girls denied doing anything wrong. When it got to my turn, and I saw the look on my caseworker's face, I knew all bets were off. I am a horrible liar. Even when I'm trying to keep a secret, it can only stay unheard until someone asks me about it because then, I won't be able to lie about the secret. As a result, it wasn't hard for my caseworker to get the answers she needed. She only had to ask about our barbecues, and I immediately told her everything. The only thing I held back on was the names of the other women, following the code of the streets. I had no intention of ratting out my crew, the people I considered family at that point in my life.

I told my caseworker that I would attend some AA meetings, as I knew it wasn't acceptable to jeopardize my family's well-being just for a good time. My caseworker wasted no time showing me how disappointed she was, deciding to talk to the board about what should be done.

For the next few days, no one would talk to me. They knew I had ratted myself out and assumed I had done the same to them. Someone poured bleach all over my clothes a day or so later. I guess someone thought I was tattling, even though I never did. They never asked, anyway.

The next day I was called back in by my caseworker. I remember being scared of what she might say about me. To my utter surprise, she told me how proud she was of me for being the only one to tell the truth, and for agreeing to go to AA meetings.

This honesty of mine made them think of giving me another chance rather than throwing me out of the shelter. However, they also made it clear that strict rules would be in place this time. I had never been more grateful than I was then because God had granted me another chance, and I was determined to take my life more seriously. After all, what was the use of learning responsibility if it wasn't practiced? I accepted what I needed to know from Bay Area Turning Point, understanding that every choice we make in our lives is meant to teach us a lesson.

I couldn't wait for the day that I could give back to the shelter that had given me so much. All shelters can use extra help, even those as great as Bay Area Turning Point. You don't always have to give money, but you can pick up an extra roll of toilet paper or paper towels, diapers, food, and clothes. All these items are bound to help your local shelter in more ways than you can imagine. You have to understand that these places provide every single need for these families, and they, in turn, need all the help they can get.

After thirty days at the shelter, I got into the transitional housing in the Pasadena area with a recommendation from my caseworker. However, there were two requirements. The first was that the resident needed a means of transportation; unfortunately, my fixer-upper Ford had recently broken down. This was terrible timing, as, without a car, I had no idea how I was going to get a place to live or how I would get to my classes on time.

The car had needed repairs before, and my church family had always stepped in. Lynn, the nurse that headed the Esther group, had her husband work on the Ford anytime there was a problem. However, this particular time, Lynn's husband worked extra hours and couldn't find time to fix my car. I was in a fix.

To my huge surprise, the two of them gave me a vehicle when I mentioned my issue to them. It was a Geo Tracker, and I immediately fell in love with it. It was green, nearly new, and awesome. Shortly after they gave it to me, I discovered they were getting this truck for me out of their own pockets. I couldn't believe it. They paid the expenses on the vehicle for a year, until I could pay it off myself. I pray for blessings over their lives, and I thank God for bringing them along my way.

The second thing I needed to move into this transitional housing was to either have a job or be enrolled in school, and I had both. There was my house cleaning business, so I had a means of income. Everything worked out so great that I felt it was moving so fast. I moved out of the shelter and into the transitional housing in the eleventh month of 2000. For the first time in a long time, I was truly happy.

The Gruesome Twosome

The "gruesome twosome" was the nickname I gave my children, Cameron and Cindy. While I loved them beyond imagination, they were out of control. Cameron and Cindy could tear up a house quicker than a New York minute. Each time I tried to get waitressing jobs during the day – something more than cleaning homes - the childcare centers tended to call me at work after the second or third day. I always had to leave work when they called because they just couldn't handle my children.

I thought that over time their behavior would settle down. How laughable the thought must have been. Coupled with that, I was also running short on money, and this fear was beginning to catch up with me. I had bills to pay and I still had to attend classes. I started to get depressed and laughing at random jokes I encountered became increasingly difficult.

After all that happened, alongside the time and effort I spent getting out of that hole, it is embarrassing to say that I started drinking again. But this time, I could limit the number of drinks, consuming only three or four bottles. It was to wind down at the end of the day. But this was no excuse. I was back to using alcohol as a tool to sedate myself from all the stress. It felt like a good escape route, regardless of my previous relationship with those bottles. I felt like I was drowning, and I believed that the drink kept me afloat.

The problems with Cameron and Cindy existed regardless of who cared for them. Cameron cried and banged his head. With me, he was always fine, but when I left him, he would be inconsolable and refuse to behave for anyone else. I cried so many times over the pain I knew he felt because I felt powerless to help him. There was nothing I could do. I couldn't be with him all the time like he wanted. I had to take care of myself too.

The rash behavior of my four-year-old son was becoming a nightmare. Cameron would constantly get into situations where he would purposefully try to hurt himself. Was he self- sabotaging at the tender age of four? I was lost as to where he got that notion from. Should I have tried harder to keep him with me after his birth? What had I done to him? I couldn't help but blame myself. After all, it wasn't his fault that I had used drugs while I was pregnant with him. I had hurt my child and I couldn't fix it. I was the one who hadn't been able to get a firm enough grip on my life. I felt unable to give my children the kind of life they deserved, one where I was always available to them, where the hardest thing they had to worry about would be deciding which cereal to have for breakfast.

I cried out to God for my son, often sobbing and aching inside. But things got so bad that I had to hospitalize him. The psychologists told me that his behavior issues were indeed his attempts of self-sabotaging himself. He was suicidal! My son was suicidal! I thought the drama in my life had come to an end. This development hit me straight in my bones. Cameron was in a children's psychiatric ward for seven days.

His sister Cindy wasn't doing well either, as she was going through a different issue. Cindy was usually loving and sweet, but sometimes she showed signs of anger problems. There were times she would swear that I had said something I never did, and I just had to accept it to get her to calm down. I loved and comforted Cindy, but I had to concentrate on Cameron. He apparently needed me more, as he kept trying to hurt himself even while in the hospital. Perhaps, my extra attention towards Cameron made Cindy feel threatened, jealous, and insecure. Maybe that created the perfect excuse necessary, worsening her anger issues. Did she feel like she never had a mommy to herself as much as her brother did?

My kids had to survive while managing their issues, but as the famous saying goes, time waits for no man. After about six months, I received public Housing and moved into a new apartment. Public Housing was different than Transitional Housing. In transitional Housing, there were strict rules concerning men and curfews, alongside meetings we had to attend. There were also weekly apartment inspections, and only women who came out of the shelter could go into transitional Housing. However, in Public Housing, it was solely your choice where you would live, and there were no strict guidelines on usage and living. I was happy to be on my own.

Although transitional Housing was a great support, we weren't allowed to have male friends over. You might be wondering how this was an issue for me. Still, even with all the things God had done for me – saving my life, paying for my college, giving me a place to live, and blessing me with two beautiful children – I still had a huge hole in my heart, and at the time, I thought this hole indicated a need for attention and love from a man. The need for a male figure, which had been there since childhood and brought me down many wrong paths over my lifetime, was rising again inside me.

It did not help that my children were getting old enough to ask about the whereabouts of their fathers. I never thought about the effects of having children out of wedlock while pregnant or when my two kids were younger, but as the years went by, I could see that it was more damaging to the children than I could have ever imagined. I realized that children communicated with each other in school and asked questions when they saw differences in their lifestyles. Of course, the fathers of their schoolmates must have come to drop them off at school, and naturally, they were only wondering why they were different.

So, the next time my children asked me where their father was, I told them they didn't have a dad but only a mother who loved them more than anything else. But nothing could satisfy a child's need for a father, and there were not enough words in the world that I could say to my children to make up for not having one. I know that some single parents take on the responsibility of both, but if you've followed my story so far, it speaks volumes. Take a look at my life and tell me if I could assume the role of both mom *and* dad to Cameron and Cindy. Most single mothers had other adults around, like aunts or grandparents, to help and give their children extra attention. But my kids had no one but me, a woman whose parenting skills still needed work. Raising children alone is just plain hard.

All I could do was tell my kids that they didn't have a dad but that they still had me. This went on for some time until someone at Cindy's daycare told her that everyone had a father and then asked Cindy about hers. How dare the caregivers at the daycare center contradict what I told my kids? I know that my flaring up at the school and also at a little girl was baseless, but still, they had no right.

Unfortunately, my little girl would not let it go. Cindy wouldn't stop bugging me about it, asking me if I was lying to her at every opportunity she got. She was only three, and her heart ached for something she would never have, a father. I couldn't blame her. Cindy and Cameron deserved to grow with a father's protection, but it was all my fault that it was this way.

So, I decided to do something about it and start dating again. This time I vowed to make it work. My attention would be on the table, and I wouldn't allow any man to waste my time. I had my children's desires and their future on the line, and that was enough motivation to get it right. I wanted a husband!

My first date was with a guy named Darren. When he came to my house, he seemed genuinely happy to meet Cameron and Cindy. The first thing out of my little girl's mouth on seeing him was, "Are you my daddy?" I was so embarrassed, I thought I was going to die.

Darren just smiled, saying nothing.

"I am so sorry," I said, looking everywhere else but his face. I am a dark-skinned girl, but I'm sure my face must have turned red.

To make matters worse, Cameron and Cindy started jumping up and down, chanting, "Our daddy! Our daddy! our daddy!" I was mortified, needing death to come at that very moment. Of course, that didn't happen. That would have been too easy. I had to suffer through every moment, wondering if I had made the right choice by bringing Darren home. All I could do was apologize.

Darren assured me it was okay, but he never called again.

The next time I went out, I ensured the guy would not meet my kids immediately. My heart hurt for my children, as I felt that the chances of finding a decent person who wanted to date someone with two children would be slim. I knew they wanted a daddy even more than I wanted a husband, but that was a turn-off.

My children's issues suddenly became more apparent, and their behavior worsened. Leaving them with sitters and at daycare was getting more difficult, as they got me out of work early, running to attend to the complaints of those in charge. They were both hard to understand, and it felt like they were doing it purposely to spite me. I thought they were being plain nasty. It took me years to realize that I was all they had; no father or visits with family members. It was just me; I was it! I was *their everything*.

I decided I couldn't blame my circumstances for preventing me from being the best parent I could possibly be to my children. I was not a good example of God's love for them, because I was too busy trying to find love for myself. So, while I was on a mission to find a father for my children, I was ignoring my Heavenly Father, making things worse by trying to fix them myself. God doesn't like it when people try to resolve issues on his behalf. There's nothing like helping God.

During these times, my mind often wandered to Hester and her relationship with Pearl. She didn't have a husband, and Pearl didn't have a father. Worse, their lives were a part of a society where the only thing women could do was hide in their husbands' shadows. If Hester could survive those circumstances, what was my excuse? Arming myself with these thoughts, I made myself a promise to hold myself more accountable for my children's well-being.

I would try harder to be the mom my kids deserve. I would give them that much.

I've often heard that parenting never comes with an instruction book, so sometimes you have to go out and buy one. And that is what I did. I started asking questions, went to parenting classes, and bought books. I began searching for the parents of well-behaved children to find out what they were doing, so I could learn by example.

I found out most of these parents were married, and that made a lot of sense. It was how God set up the family to be; a joint effort in raising children. It was only logical that it would be easier if you followed God's plan.

There was nothing I could do about being a single mother, but I had to rethink some of the things I did with my children that weren't working. After all, they were created by God and came from me. Why wouldn't I want something from myself to be good? Other parents said that children do what they see their parents doing. I needed to be a better example. So, I decided the first thing I would do was find a good job. Something more stable would afford me quality time to spend with Cindy and Cameron.

I also began to read the books on parenting that I had purchased. Every one of them strongly advised setting a schedule, so I put together a detailed routine for my children. It started from the time they woke and went through the day until bedtime. It took a couple of weeks for us to learn and imbibe the schedule, but things started to turn around when we did. Even my behavior began improving. I wasn't as stressed out as I had been over everything, and I didn't feel the need to drink anymore. This year, my children and I began to flourish as a family. I no longer called my children the gruesome twosome. They had now become a dynamic duo.

20

Job Hunt vs. Husband Hunt

As much as I loved the Lord and my children, at 27, I felt something was still missing in my life. It was a recurring thought and feeling at almost every turn I took, like when I tried to reach something from the topmost part of the kitchen cupboards or at nights when I held my pillows tightly to myself. I assumed that my need was the most obvious thing, as my being single kept messing with my mind. It couldn't have been anything else. My children were fantastic. Cameron and Cindy made me laugh and kept me from wanting to do drugs; I wanted to see them happy and healthy. Was it a need for something more fulfilling? I also felt like I needed something for myself, something that could make me feel self-substantial. This need made me begin to look for a different job. I was blessed by the houses I cleaned, but I longed to do something more meaningful. But what could I do? I didn't have any talents that I knew of.

I had an interview with a local food chain for a management position, and it went very well. I was essentially promised the job as long as I passed the background check. But of course, I couldn't pass a background check. As expected, each of my arrests came up when the check was run. The worst thing on the list was prostitution. Although I tried to explain to the district manager that the case was dismissed due to a mistaken identity and that the whole thing had nothing to do with me, he remained adamant about his conclusion. The district manager mentioned that it was there on my background-raised issues, and he would not be hiring me because of it. I began to get depressed again, wanting to rip this letter off my chest and remove the mark of Cain from my head. It had a mix of anger embedded somewhere, as I was so upset that I had to suffer for events that I wasn't guilty of, dismissed or not.

The thought of never being able to get a decent job broke my heart. It felt as if there was a glass roof above my head, and I would never be able to break through it. I began to think that if maybe I could find true love, I wouldn't have to worry as much about having a significant career. It seemed like the perfect solution for me. If I can't get one, why not try the other?

I continued to go on dates with different guys. My neighbor Connie agreed to help keep my children, so being out at night was easier without worrying about them. For the most part, the kids behaved on these nights. It helped that I would wait until after bedtime to go out, stealing goodnight kisses from Cameron and Cindy after they'd fallen asleep. It was a perfect arrangement and worked most of the time.

I started seeing Mike regularly. He was a single father with a daughter, and I thought it sexy to see a guy finding courage and taking good care of his daughter by himself. Mike and I got along great, except he liked to flirt with other women in front of me. I didn't hold on to that trait because I didn't see us lasting long. The red flags were waving with such ferocity. I later learned that he did the same thing to his ex-girlfriend, who was currently in jail. I hung out with Mike for about six months, but when he told me his baby's mama was getting out of jail, and he was going to be with her, it didn't even have to be said that things between us were now over.

But unexpectedly, Mike told me that his ex-girlfriend was bisexual and "would really like me." At that moment, I saw what he was hinting at.

"Mike," I said. "Do you seriously believe that the three of us together are going to be one big happy family? Can you hear yourself speak?"

"I was hoping we could," Mike said with a huge grin on his face.

I just stared incredulously at him. Like it could happen. My kids, his kid, his baby mama, himself, and me? Jerk! What a chauvinistic move! But despite this, I liked Mike's friends. They were young, successful, and had promising futures. I wanted these things too. As much as I enjoyed my church friends, they were older and married, with other married friends to keep them company, and I didn't exactly fit into that space. Connie had become my best friend, as she shared my habit of dating the wrong men. Laughable, isn't it? But the bond we both shared transcended into our separate lives. At this point in my life, God had thankfully taken away my addiction to drugs and partying.

However, I still had issues about wanting to feel loved at any cost. I wanted to be enough for someone, to have someone tell me that I was loved. I had a God-given need that satan perverted. I hated being lonely and unmarried. It made me feel inadequate.

Meanwhile, I continued the job hunt and took a job at the Waffle House. The Waffle House wanted me to be a shift manager, but the hours were terrible, and I just couldn't leave my children at night anymore after the plethora of badly ended dates. If I were to take it, I would also have to quit school, and that was not an option. If I left school, there was no doubt that I would always have to struggle.

I decided to apply when someone told me there were openings in the Houston school district for substitute teachers. It was the job of my dreams, a professional job I could be proud of, one my children would be able to respect. I applied for the position but ended up not getting the job. I assumed that the background check and my limited job history had something to do with it. It was always there waiting to stab me in the back.

The Universe again reminded me that my background would remain my scarlet letter, announcing to everyone that I was not to be trusted and scaring everybody away before I had a chance to prove myself otherwise. It was something I had to live with, as I wasn't sure when I would be free from its chains.

Not being able to get a job did not make me feel good about myself, but I had to keep trying. Giving up wasn't an option. My mother had raised us to be independent, and I, the oldest, was the only one who could not catch a break. After all, God forgave me and let me go to college. If He was on my side, no one could be against me. Whenever I felt hope beginning to leave my heart, I would remind myself of God's love and support. He already took me away from so much misery. Indeed, He must have also considered the rest of my journey. God wasn't one to halt in the middle of a journey.

I regularly reminded myself of this as I worked on improving my life. They say that you don't need anyone else when you have God by your side. And if He was indeed on my side, these hard times were just a hiccup. Determination had become my new best friend. Little did I know how much assistance I would need from this new friend later.

21

A Marriage Made in Hell

The scarlet letter on my chest made staying positive and determined very difficult. The more I tried to tear it off, the more the adhesive stuck to me. No matter where I went, my past was at my tail. There was no detaching it in sight.

The job hunt continued terribly, and I went on at least eight interviews in a row without a single callback. The worse part of it all was waiting for my phone to ring from where it sat on the center stool in my living room. There was nothing else to do but sit there, hopeful but knowing that my chances were slim. Some companies were nice enough to send me a postcard, saying, "Thanks for applying, but we have filled the position." I knew what they meant to say was, "Thanks for applying. You gave us a good laugh, but don't bother coming back. We aren't interested in people like you."

At least that's what it felt like. It made me wonder if anyone would ever forgive me for making a two-year mistake in my life. Or would this bad luck never end? Would I have to trudge on in this plight?

While wallowing in self-pity over my failed attempts at finding employment, I was still hanging out with friends of Mike, the single father with the wandering eye and locked-up girlfriend. They also became my friends during the period we dated, and we remained friends even after Mike and I were finished. One day, when we were all hanging out at a pool hall, I saw a guy that caught my attention. Our eyes connected, and I knew I needed to talk to him in those few seconds, and he wanted to talk to me too.

He couldn't take his eyes off me, his beautiful stares eating me up from within. I wanted to put my hands all over him, feeling what lay underneath the lumber jacket was wearing. He kept staring from where he stood, not making any move to cover the short distance between us. By this time, my determination and assertive attitude applied to the job hunt and my hunt for a husband, and I couldn't wait for him to make the first move.

On my way to get another drink, I walked straight up to him and asked, "Are you ever going to say something to me? You seem content with just staring."

"Aren't you with Mike?" He asked in a deep masculine tone. Everybody thought that because I still hung out with Mike's crew.

"I am trying to get with you," I responded, playing with my hair. "Good pick-up line, huh?"

We both started laughing, and after a while, my friends wanted to know what was so damn funny.

"I've never had a chick throw *me* a pick-up line before." He said, seemingly fascinated by my approach.

We laughed some more.

"So, you're not with Mike," he said cautiously. "Or are you just pulling my leg?"

"Nah," I responded, shaking my head slowly. "But he did offer to move me in with his baby mama, who just got out of jail."

"What?" He said, his eyes widening in disbelief.

"Nope, we're definitely not dating anymore!" It called for a good laugh. "Do you have any baby mamas in jail anywhere?"

"Nope." He replied automatically.

"Girlfriends, wives?"

"I have only had two girlfriends, and that was years ago," he said, angling his head to see where I was headed with my questions.

"How old are you?"

"27."

"Me too," I said, wanting him to know that I wasn't too young or too old. "So, you mean to tell me that you are 27 and you don't have any children?"

"Nah, no children," he replied, shaking his head. "I don't think I can have any. I want some, though."

Poor guy didn't even know those were the magic words! He was starting to look even better to me. He introduced himself as Matthew, and the more we talked, the more he seemed like a real catch. He was easy to converse with and always wanted to listen to what I had to say. I told Matthew about my children, and he said he couldn't wait to meet them. I was usually nervous about bringing others around my family because I knew Cameron and Cindy would give anyone a run for their money. It had happened so many times before. Well, I thought to myself, he wasn't the man for me if they scared him off. The man of my dreams would always have to get my children's approval, as they were an indispensable part of me.

Matthew admitted he had seen me before, and a mutual friend told him I was Mike's girl. I laughed when I realized who the "mutual friend" was. It was Brian, another friend who had wanted to get with me for as long as I could remember. Brian had known that Mike and I had broken up, but he probably was afraid of ruining his own chances. When I explained this to Matthew, we had a good laugh. Later, we exchanged phone numbers and set up a date.

I was so excited about my upcoming date, but I kept wondering if Matthew was as cute as I remembered. He was a Latino man with a brown glow and a broad, muscular chest. I loved his looks, but I wasn't sure if it was just the state of my mind on the day we met that had heightened his looks for me.

A few days later, when I met him for our anticipated date, I realized he was even better looking than I had initially thought! It was love at first sight! Or was it lust? Either way, I was incredibly attracted to him. Matthew was funny and sounded pleasant when he laughed. We played pool for a while and returned to my house for a few cans of beer. I figured it was okay since my children were asleep. We never once talked about God, our beliefs, or what we wanted out of life. We just slept together, our attraction taking the forefront in our union. I told myself he was the one, but I was settling. I wanted a man who was available and very interested in me, so I went for him – even though I knew it was wrong.

The following day, Cindy met me in my room. Usually, I was careful enough to ensure any man who stayed the night would be gone by the time my children awoke. But I wasn't that careful this time. Cindy entered my room and found Matthew sprawled on the bed, covered midway with my white sheets. She had a million and one questions for him, including the dreadful, "Are you my daddy?" I was sure this would be the last time I would ever see Matthew. But to my surprise, he just laughed extremely hard. Cindy just stood there, waiting for the answer she never got.

After that day, Matthew became a part of our family. Cindy fell in love with him just like I did; he wove his life around us seamlessly and beautifully. Or so I thought. Matthew was usually playful with the kids and so helpful that he seemed so perfect. But around the house, he had an ugly side as well.

The closer you get to people, the more you see them as they truly are. It's funny that they often turn out to be so different than you want them to be. I soon got to know that Matthew had a drinking problem. Anytime he drank too much, he would become terrifying, with violent outbursts that frightened me, Cindy, and Cameron. Matthew would also destroy things around the house, particularly things that my family had given to me. I would throw him out of the home, but the next day he would return full of apologies and claims that he couldn't remember what had happened the night before. Matthew would say he missed the kids and claimed that he hadn't done well while he'd been away from them. To further weaken my resolve, Cindy would cry for him, having grown as attached to him as she was to me. I would always cave in and give him another chance because I wanted to believe that he could become the husband and father I wanted so badly.

I dreamed of a perfect family, with a husband who took care of my children, brought home flowers, and, most importantly, one who loved us unconditionally. I hoped that giving him another chance would allow Matthew to become the kind of man I had dreamt about. And I hoped I wasn't making another mistake.

I loved Matthew, and I always wanted to believe that he would change for us, for the family he was getting. Cindy and Cameron inspired me to change, and I wanted to believe that the three of us could do the same for Matthew.

I failed to see that Cindy and Cameron made me change because they were of the same blood as me. But there was no way Matthew would share that same kind of bond. He was different.

Like any other woman in love, desperate to find affection in a man who was a lost cause, I tried to change Matthew. He would make promises to behave differently, and I wanted to believe him, just like my mom had done for my dad after his Friday-night outbursts. At that moment, the end of that story ceased to mean anything to me.

But just like my father, Matthew never changed. You should understand that you are deceiving yourself if you are waiting for a guy to change his ways or feel that your love for him will somehow be reason enough for him to change. Over the years, I have realized that actual change comes when people intentionally desire to change their ways, not when someone else wants them to do so.

For women who are hurt by the men they are in love with, remember that ultimately it is a man's actions, not his words, which you must consider. A man's pretty words and empty promises will do little for you, but they have the potential to leave you with nothing, emptying you of the emotions and passion you held on to.

Still, I was desperate to have a man in my life and a father for my kids. Through my church and on my own, I had been reading the Bible regularly. One passage from *2 Corinthians* ran through my mind as I thought about Matthew, "Do not be yoked together with unbelievers, for what do righteousness and wickedness have in common?(*2 Corinthians 6:14*)"

I knew that God was telling me not to stay with Matthew, as he was in no way exhibiting signs of a righteous man. It was apparent in the lies he told and the actions he took. As a woman daily striving to be righteous, I should have fled from a man who was not interested in seeking a better path. But I couldn't get my mind right. I felt I needed someone to love me, and that someone had to be Matthew.

Although it was clear that we had very different ideas about how a family should behave, when I got pregnant, we decided to get married. I was tired of having children out of wedlock, and I certainly did not want to have another abortion. So, there was no other option than to get married to Matthew. And while I was busy preparing to be a wife to him, I flunked out of school.

I prayed for God to show me Matthew's heart, and He did, even though it wasn't what I wanted or expected. In response to my prayers, Matthew disappeared right before our wedding. But that wasn't what I meant! I wanted God to show me the good in Matthew, but apparently, God thought it was better that I saw Matthew for what he really was. His disappearance before the ceremony was disappointing, but it wasn't the only time Matthew would suddenly be absent. He would pop in and out of my life without any explanation or apology.

But I was stubborn and needy, afraid of being alone again, especially because I had three children now. Overlooking Matthew's faults and God's unmistakable message, I married him anyway. My fear of being alone was more profound than my trust in the Lord.

Every part of our relationship and marriage was stressful, especially while I was pregnant. I thought being pregnant would make Matthew straighten his ways, but things did not improve. I was not making enough money, and Matthew was an unreliable source of income. He often didn't work, and when he did manage to find a job, he would disappear on each payday. While he was away, he would miss work and lose the job, resuming the cycle all over again. My family was more extensive, but I was overwhelmed and couldn't make ends meet. How would I be able to fulfill God's plan for my life?

My life was going so poorly again, and I became certain that it was because I had messed up badly. I feared that I would never fulfill my potential as God had intended. I often prayed for the Lord to show my husband's heart throughout my marriage. Each time I prayed this prayer for God to show me his heart, Matthew would disappear for a day, two even two weeks. It soon became apparent that it was God my heart longed for. Only God could bring healing to the wounded parts of my heart. Not a man who lacked in more ways than I could count. My heart needed a perfect being, and there was no one like that on earth.

GOD'S PURPOSE:
What He Really Wanted from Me

We wonder about our purpose in this world at specific points in life. We ask questions that border along the lines of purpose, direction, and self-worth. Is our existence meaningless? Is there more to our identity? Sometimes it takes years or even decades for some meaning to find its way to us. And even when we find it, we don't always know what to do with it. The sense of wanting to prove ourselves hovers around our heads like a rope for a suicide attempt, but we just stare at it, clueless.

It can take months or years before that purpose is even a possibility. When I was young, God showed me that I would fulfill my purpose by ministering to thousands of young people. I believed it then, but as my life took me in so many wrong directions, I lost sight of that purpose. I barely even remembered it amidst dancing, getting pregnant, the drugs...it was all but gone from sight.

But God did not forget. He never does.

After failing out of college, giving birth to two more children, and still being unable to find a decent job, life looked particularly grim. I was tired of cleaning houses and waiting tables. I knew I had made a mess of things and had ruined the chance at college that God had so carefully arranged for me, and it was tough for me to ask Him for another favor. But I hoped that He could still use me in some way. I hoped I wasn't a cast away just yet.

I was asking a lot, considering all of my failures were my own fault. The signs were glaring, lighting up like neon lights in my head, yet I chose to ignore them repeatedly. God even told me not to marry Matthew, but I did it anyway! What do you call that?

What was I going to do about my life now? It seemed too late to start steering my ship onto the path of discovery and self-realization all over again. Although I was ready to make a change and put my life back in God's hands, it was all such a mess. My children were having major behavioral issues again. Cindy even heard voices now, crying so loud each time it happened. I took her to a psychiatrist who diagnosed her with bipolar disorder. My poor baby! I couldn't feel like this was all my doing, as I had no control over her nature. But in a way, it was.

I needed a job. Ms. Lynn had resigned as the head of our single mom's group because of some family issues that had to be addressed, leaving me without my source of guidance and release. To top it off, my husband was crazy, acting like he did not care for any of us. I felt like my whole world was caving in, and I was going to break at any second. I couldn't see a plan for my life anywhere. It was chaos at every turn until God gave me peace.

Generally, my communication with God involved asking a question, and in each of those times, God always gave me an answer, even if it always turned out to be a no. At other times God gave me a command without asking first, such as the time he told me to go to school and when he told me I had to make a choice.

This time, however, the message was more subtle and came through Connie, one of His servants, who also was my friend. It was one of the few times He spoke to me through another human.

One day, Connie told me she had just gotten a job with a school in Houston. I was happy for her, but I was also envious because I was having such a difficult time getting a respectable job while she had it easy. I had really wanted to work as a substitute teacher and was incredibly disappointed when my background check prevented me from being hired. So, it was difficult for me not to feel slighted, even though Connie was usually friendly to me. I was trying to find a re-direction, and having someone do it so seamlessly and right in my face wasn't doing much to my morale.

Connie had always been open and honest with me, so I told her about my issues with the background check. She looked at me and said, "Everyone makes mistakes Tyra, as they cannot be expunged from our daily living. But I know for certain that you are not a felon. Call up there and make an appointment to see the head of human resources. Explain the situation. The worst they can do is say no. That wouldn't do as much as cut your skin, would it?"

"No," I replied, shaking my head in disagreement. "The worst thing they can do is kick me out and file a restraining order."

But in truth, I ended up taking Connie's advice anyway. It was the least I could do for myself and my children, who seemed to have no other source of support and love.

When I called human resources, they told me to send in an application. I explained to them that I had already applied two years prior but was never hired. The woman on the line was understanding and helpful, as she checked my previous application and found I was denied employment due to a negative background check. This came as no surprise to me. She asked me if I would like to speak to the head of human resources, and I said that I would. Honestly, I thought it would end up like the last application, so my hopes weren't high.

The woman connected my call to Mr. Mannis, the head of human resources. His loud voice booming through my phone speaker said, "Mannis here. How may I help you?"

I explained that I had previously applied for the post of substitute teacher but had not been hired because of a negative background check. I was honest about everything to Mr. Mannis. I told him I knew I had messed up in the past, but I was no longer that person, as that had been such a long time ago. I wanted the opportunity to work for his district. It would be a dream come true. I also explained how the charge of prostitution was a mistaken identity charge, and the charges had been dropped during the time of the arrest. It was all a mix-up that had continued to haunt me ever since.

"Well," Mr. Mannis said, the tone of his voice lowering a notch. "I need you to fill out another application. This time I need you to list every offense and arrest you have ever had. After you submit your application, check at the front to see the status of your application." He was polite, and there was no sign of judgment in his voice. I think he believed me.

"Thank you, sir, I will."

I wasn't sure if I wanted to go through with the application or not, as I was scared of being rejected yet again. I told myself to overcome this fear and weakness, to stop them from running my life. They made me feel helpless and insufficient. Gathering the will and courage I needed, I went to human resources immediately and got an application before I could convince myself not to do it. I listed every arrest, and without enough room to explain them, I had to conclude it on the back of the application form.

I thought these people would tear this thing up in my face. I was afraid I would never get a decent job and would be doomed to a life of welfare. But I wanted so much more for myself and my children that the thought of failing sent me into depression more than failing itself.

The week after I spoke to Mr. Mannis, I received a postcard inviting me to a substitute orientation. Unsure of how to interpret this, I called human resources. The person on the other end of the receiver explained that I wasn't hired yet and that postcards were mailed out before background checks were completed. I was glad that I had already made it further than the last time. But still, I hadn't gotten to the point I was aiming at, high hopes or not.

A few days later, I was getting ready to attend the orientation. I was excited about it, telling Cameron how I thought it would be a door opener for us all. Although I didn't have good interviewing clothes, I remembered a nice outfit my mother had given me a while back, so I washed and ironed it. As I went to the closet to search for accessories to go with it, the strangest thing happened.

I became aware of some familiar symptoms. I ran to the full-length mirror in the bathroom, wondering if it could be what I was thinking. One pregnancy test later, I learned that sure enough, I was pregnant again. This would be my fourth child ever and second with Matthew. Don't get me wrong. I loved babies, especially each of my children. But how could I afford to raise another one with all that had been going on? Things with Matthew were not going well, but my relationship with the Lord was growing strong. So, I resorted to the only thing I knew how to do well, praying hard for my family and my husband. I hoped God would change Matthew's heart and deliver him from his deep-seated anger. I longed for him to love us as a father and husband, and I just hoped God would make everything better.

But in fact, things only got worse.

While things were rocky with family life, I managed to start the job as a substitute teacher. My first assignment was at a junior high school. From the moment I walked through the school door, I felt this was where I was supposed to be. Everything felt right, just as it had been with my college application. It was one of the best days of my life.

There was something else I realized about this school. It was in a neighborhood I used to know so well. I used to go to school in this district many years back. But things in the area had changed, and it was no longer predominately white. Back then, it almost seemed like KKK headquarters, with a very minimal amount of blacks who struggled to get through each day without any form of bullying or attack. Now though, almost all the students were Hispanic.

While I was glad that the school was no longer under the run of the KKK, it still had severe problems. The school now had gangs, and the students talked back to teachers. I was someone who understood the chip-on-my-shoulder routine, and although I was excited to be there, I was worried that I wouldn't be able to relate to the school's changing demographics. The kids weren't quiet in classrooms anymore and they said whatever they thought, good or bad. It was like I was plunged into different surroundings from the one I was used to, and I only hoped that I would be able to adapt to the striking changes quickly.

For the next six months, I traveled around the city, working in different classrooms at different schools. During that time, I had some free time between classes and was able to do a lot of reading. Teen books were my favorite, but only the fantasy ones. I wouldn't say I liked love stories because they seemed full of false hope, and I'd had enough of that to last me a lifetime.

But fantasy books provided great stories without any real possibility that they could happen. Given my own story, we all know that love stories don't come true.

At one of the schools, I worked at, one female student always gave me a hard time when she saw me. She was a pretty young lady, but it was as if the Lord had just shown me her heart. Their teacher left a writing assignment for her class, and I read over this girl's work and realized she had so much talent stored up, so I called her to stay after class. Naturally, she thought that she was in trouble. The student was very shocked to hear what I had to say.

"This is good writing," I said, sampling her submission. "Let me tell you something. Nothing is more powerful than being beautiful and smart, as those two make an unstoppable combination. Quit playin' and take care of your business."

She stared at me in silence for a minute before saying, "Thanks, miss, I'll try harder." I was pretty surprised she even listened to me.

The next day I was working in the same school and was pregnant with my last child. This girl that had given me so much trouble for the last couple of days stopped me in the hall and asked me, "Have you got a name for your baby yet?"

I angled my head, wondering why she was suddenly interested. "No, not really."

"Is it a girl or a boy?" She questioned.

"It's a girl." I sighed, asking myself when the interrogation was going to end. I still wasn't comfortable talking about something unplanned.

"Are you happy?"

"Oh yeah!" I replied. I had gotten pregnant just three months after I gave birth to my last child. While I was happy about birthing another cute creature, I was scared too. I didn't know how we were going to survive the extra mouth.

I returned to the class I was teaching, handing out the lesson that the teacher had left for her class. It was a better day with this set of students, as they seemed preoccupied with something other than disturbances. At the end of the period, this young lady I had had so much trouble with handed me a sheet of paper. A list of twenty-five names for baby girls was on the sheet of paper. I was touched by her gesture.

One of those names became the middle name of my baby girl, Kara. In fact, it was nearly her first name until I had a dream one night where the Lord told me to name her Annalisa. Was the dream a message from God? I'm still unsure, but it didn't seem like something I should take a chance on.

I loved my work and students like the one who gave me that list of baby names. It was great because I felt I was making a difference with my work. Being a substitute teacher was excellent. It was the best job I had ever had, making me feel relevant with all the help I was rendering. There was my self-fulfillment.

23

Good Things Come to Those Who Wait

Summer was around the corner, and while I loved being a substitute teacher, I needed something more permanent. The break would come with unemployment, and that in turn meant no pay coming in. The kids were more demanding now than ever, and no income just didn't work. Now that I had spent more time in school, I had a better concept of how things worked, and my employability status had boosted a little bit. I thought that being an employee would give me a better chance of getting a full-time job. I hoped to be hired as a paraprofessional, also referred to as a teacher's aide. I loved being a substitute because it allowed me to interact with students at various age levels and different schools. But I longed to work in a position where I would have a more lasting impact. Seeing the same students daily would give me that chance, not just an occasional sub that was not always needed.

Staff members at the schools seemed so full of purpose. As they say, the grass is always greener on the other side. Their lawns looked almost tropical to me. I thought I would be much happier if I had a full-time position, regardless of the level or students. All that mattered to me was the position. At nights, I would toss on my bed, thinking about what I should do next as regards the school I worked at. I wasn't sure I would find a suitable full-time position, but still, I put my faith in God. Although I knew that the sins of my past could hinder my ability to get a stable, respectable job, I was hoping that wouldn't apply here, at least, for the sake of my children.

After my worries got me nowhere, I decided to call the head of the paraprofessionals. Ms. Gamboa was the one to go to if anyone was interested in an aide job. I was nervous and even a little bit afraid, preoccupied with the notion that they might realize that I should never have been hired as a substitute in the first place. But if I wanted a permanent position, I had to make this call. So, I chucked in my fears at the deepest part of my system, swallowed deeply, and picked up my phone.

"Ms. Gamboa., good morning.," I greeted, trying to sound bright and excited. "My name is Tyra. I am a substitute teacher in the district, and I was hoping for a more permanent position." I crossed my fingers underneath the local pamphlet I had read before placing the call.

"So, you already work for our district?" She asked, going straight to the point. I was hoping she would return my greetings. Now, this only made me more scared.

"Yes, ma'am," I replied, swallowing again. I could feel an increase in the pace of my heartbeat.

"Tell me your name again, please?" She sounded detached.

I told her my full name and I could hear the clicks of a keyboard as she typed something in the background. I held onto the phone anxiously, waiting for news that could either make a future or break my heart. There was a loud shriek getting into my head, and I knew I was the only one who could hear it. It came with anxiety.

"Ms. Wilson, all we need now is a current resume and a letter of interest. Then I can put you on the list." Mrs. Gambia said politely. I noticed the change in her tone, presumably after she read something about me after she typed out my name.

"Which list is that?" I questioned, oblivious to the existence of anything of that nature.

"The list that tells schools they can hire you, that you are a suitable choice." She explained slowly.

"And that's it? I am hired?" It sounded unbelievable.

"Well, Ms. Wilson, you still have to attend an interview when a school calls, and of course, you should understand that there are many names before yours on the list."

I nodded, even though she could not see me. That was how the system was run.

I quickly turned in the required material and continued to call Ms. Gamboa, first to ensure I had been put on the list and then to see if I had moved up. I knew it would take some time, but a little asking around could do no harm. After my sixth or seventh call, it was pretty apparent that I was very eager for a job. Ms. Gamboa warned me that the starting salary was only about twelve to thirteen thousand dollars a year, but I couldn't care less. I wanted to work around other professional types and wasn't concerned about the pay. At least, not for now. Later I realized that I needed that job nearly as much as that job required a person like me.

Two weeks passed, and I still hadn't heard from any schools. Was I looking at rejection in the face again? I mean, it was something I couldn't help but expect.

Panicking, I called Ms. Gamboa's office again, making her aware of my concerns and asking if there was a way to communicate my interest personally to these schools rather than waiting for their call. She reminded me that I was way down on the list and would have to be patient, but she gave me some excellent advice on acing an interview.

She even invited me to do a mock interview with her as the interviewer.

"When you get into the office that has been arranged for the interview," she said on the day we agreed to meet. "Introduce yourself to everyone in the room before you get seated. Bring extra resumes, so you have one for each person."

I nodded with rapt attention as she gave several more pointers. Probably the most helpful tip she gave was to send a resume to every school where I wanted to work. So that's what I did. I sent a resume to all 68 schools in the district, detailing that I would accept any kind of position.

I waited a week before I received my first phone call. I was called for an interview at an intermediate school, and four other individuals were in the meeting. The interview didn't go very well for me because I wasn't confident and failed to portray myself as a leader. The least I could do for myself was to be conscious of all my mistakes and honest about where the fault was. All I had practiced during the mock interview with Ms. Gamboa evaporated from my mind.

I thought it would be wrong to come off as a know-it-all, so when asked about being a leader, I said, "I am a follower because leaders need someone to follow." I closed my eyes for a second when I was done spitting out that nonsense. Why did I say that?

As soon as I answered the question, I could see the expressions of the interviewer change. I knew I had blown my chances with what I had just said. Long story short, they never called. There was no way they were going to call anyway. What was I thinking? It was a pretty stupid comment, but I didn't know what I was doing and wanted to say the right things so badly. I had no idea it would turn into the opposite.

I figured the district would send a message to other schools through their phone grapevine to not hire this crazy girl. I replayed the interview in my mind so many times, and every time I did, a new wave of embarrassment would crash over me. It was like I had zoned out when the question was asked and only returned the moment I was done answering.

Another school called about an interview, and I was relieved that my initial fear wasn't the case. I addressed their questions better this time, but they feared I would hurt myself since I was pregnant. The students would be difficult to handle because of their disabilities, and the school thought it would be too much for a pregnant woman. I completely understood their concerns, but it wasn't very reassuring, nevertheless. It was just another failed attempt on my person record.

There were no more phone calls for the rest of the summer. I was surprised because I figured that with 58 resumes out there, statistics would have been on my side. But then, there was the list on which my name was at the bottom of.

The summer was brutal. I had no income other than the SSI from Cindy's disabilities. I still received food stamps, and although that helped a lot, it was very unpleasant to apply for. Sometimes people in the office made me feel like I was lazy or less of an American. And no matter how much I wanted to talk back or hurl some hurtful words in return, I had to deal with it because I knew that without them, we would have starved.

At home, things continued to deteriorate, like my efforts only bounced off the walls. Cindy had frequent violent outbursts, and Matthew would disappear often and had his own violent outbursts whenever he was around. My life was incredibly stressful, and I prayed all summer for just one more phone call, but no calls ever came. I ran in haste each time I heard my phone ring, but it always ended up being Matthew calling to complain about something or the hospital where Cindy was being treated.

The end of the summer finally came, and I received a postcard from the school district. They wanted to know if I would sub again, and of course, I did. The option was to either accept that or remain without a means of employment. If this was what God had for me, I would be happy to do it. I still wanted a paraprofessional position, but I would be grateful for whatever God saw fit to give me.

I called the district to let them know I wanted to continue substitute teaching during the upcoming school year.

All subs for the next school year were required to attend a day of training, and I didn't mind going. In fact, I looked forward to visiting different schools and doing all the reading I would be able to that year. I had already made a list of all the books I wanted to read, not to mention having the money to pay for them.

Matthew was waiting for me when I came home, a rare occurrence. I instantly knew something was up. Excitedly, he wasted no time in giving me a phone message. "A school called and wanted to know if you could come for an interview," he said.

"Quit playin'," I responded, rolling my eyes and heading to the bedroom.

Matthew pulled me right back. "Right hand to the man." He always kissed the tips of his finger and held them up in the air when trying to prove he was telling the truth.

I grabbed the paper out of his hand. It read Mr. Carnes. That meant it was for an intermediate school and not for elementary. That was a relief. I called Mr. Carnes immediately and set up an interview for the next day.

I began to pray, "Lord, please put the right words in my mouth and put me in the right position." I knew firsthand how easy it was to lose a out on job opportunity with a single mistake. The following day arrived, and I looked super pregnant. There was no way to hide it, with my plump self-trying to fit into a slim dress. There was no way they would hire me, knowing I would need maternity leave immediately. I could only convince them that I was more than qualified, and the thought sounded like a challenging task.

I felt nervous during the interview. Classes would begin in two days, and it was unlikely that I would have another chance if I lost this one. A huge watermelon sticking out of my abdomen was another excuse for them to not hire me. As I checked in with the school's front office, I remembered that this school had been our rival when I was in junior high school. That brought back memories of being young and stupid and, in my case, idiotically insane.

In junior high, I recall being ineligible to play on any sports team because of my failing grades. This memory made me begin to doubt myself again.

What in the world was I doing at this place?

I was greeted by a handsome, sharply dressed man with shiny shoes that I couldn't take my eyes off of. "Hello, Ms. Wilson," he said in a base tone. "I'm Mr. Carnes."

I slowly lifted myself out of my seat and followed Mr. Carnes into an office where another man was already waiting. The man glanced at me quickly, then returned his eyes to the sheet of paper in front of him. As the interview started, my confidence began to rise. At first, the two men seemed less interested in discussing my background and more about programs at their school.

One program was for the mentally challenged, which is the one I assumed I would be working in. The second program was a behavioral program for emotionally disturbed students. They asked me if I had any background knowledge regarding these types of disabilities.

"Actually," I replied, "that is what I went to school for. I received a certificate in mental health, although I have not finished my bachelor's degree yet."

That caught their attention.

"I have studied mental disorders as well as substance abuse," I continued, gaining more confidence from their seemingly growing interest. "I also have a daughter diagnosed with bipolar disorder, and she hears voices. She's too young to be diagnosed with schizophrenia, but the signs all point to that."

"Ms. Wilson, what can you tell me about a kid who is an average student and is consistently late but never gives the teachers any problems? He has had over 60 absences during the school year but always attends after-school detention?"

"Mr. Carnes, right?" I looked quizzically, and the man who asked the question nodded. "There can be many factors, so you can't always go by first impressions. The fact that he passes his classes shows that he does care about his grades. I'm not racially profiling, but is he Hispanic?"

"Yes, ma'am," I stopped for a second, not used to people addressing me this way.

"Have you followed him home and to school?" I inquired, curious about this riddle.

"Yes," Mr. Carnes answered. "He lives in town, very close." He seemed to be enamored by what I was saying.

"We followed him home," the second man added.

"I would also follow him to school," I continued after listening to their replies. "Just because he goes somewhere after school doesn't mean he lives there. It might just be a holding place. Also, is he staying up late playing video games or on a medication that keeps him from sleeping?" My mind went back to the occurrence a few years ago at night when I checked on Cameron and found him wide awake in the dark, just staring at the ceiling. It had freaked me out.

The interviewers were hanging on to my every word, so I kept talking, responding to the questions as they kept throwing more in. I was ready with a seasoned response to every question, and at the end of the interview, the two principals wanted to know which program I would be interested in applying for.

The answer seemed clear, so I said, "I am interested in the adaptive behavior program."

"Okay, Ms. Wilson, we have a couple more interviews to conduct, and then we will get back to you." That was not what I wanted to hear.

It was not what I was expecting after my brilliant performance there. I desperately wanted a job at this school, so I began talking. I knew I had to make a stronger case.

"Thank you so much for your time, but please, don't avoid hiring me because I'm pregnant," I knew I was pulling their attention to something they had not referred to throughout the interview, but I felt that it was necessary. "I have been promoted or at least offered a promotion at every job I can remember. I am loyal and hard-working. This will also be my fourth child, and with each of the other three, I came back to work only two weeks after I gave birth, so you don't have to worry about that. Just give me a chance."

I wasn't sure if this was professional, but I knew that my pregnancy must have been something they had noticed and had to consider. I needed to address these concerns head-on.

I left, not sure what was going to happen. On my way out, I saw another seated woman waiting to be interviewed. She was an older woman, probably in her late sixties or early seventies. She looked stern, as if she would swat students on the hands with a ruler. I knew she was after my job and hoped she wasn't the type of person they were looking for. You could call it selfishness, but I could tell this was my job. I didn't want anyone else getting it.

I went home and waited for a phone call all afternoon, which didn't come. I was getting off on the wrong foot with my unborn baby already because I felt it was her fault that the phone wasn't ringing. In my mind, the blame rolled in because if it weren't for this baby, I would have been a perfect candidate for the job. I knew I was.

The following day, I lay on the couch and refused to move. I was sad, frustrated, and very pregnant. Finally, the phone rang. I could see on the Caller ID that it was the school I had interviewed at the day before, so I jumped up and cleared my throat before picking up.

"This is Tyra," I said slowly, not sounding like I had actually been waiting for the call. The last thing an employer needed to see was desperation.

"Good morning, Ms. Wilson, this is Mr. Carnes." Of course, I knew it was him. "I am calling to offer you a position."

"Yes, of course!" I replied, rubbing my plump belly. I was sorry I blamed my baby.

"Are you able to start tomorrow?" He questioned.

"Yes, and what program will I be working in?"

"You said you were interested in the adaptive behavior program."

"Yes, sir, that's the one I was hoping for." Although I wanted to work in that program, I would have accepted any other position.

I hung up the phone. "Yes!" I began to dance around the apartment, singing at the top of my voice. My family thought I had lost it. I was so happy, even happier than when I became a substitute.

"Thank you, Lord, thank you!" God was indeed faithful to the end.

I started work the next day. The students weren't there yet, as the school calendar demanded them to arrive the next day. I could hardly contain my excitement as the peer facilitator took me on tour around the school. She was so kind and patient as she introduced me to all the staff, including my new supervisor, Mr. Man. He was tall and athletic, with a voice that seemed to echo around the rooms.

I wanted to do a great job. I hadn't had meaningful employment since I was 19 when I worked at the world's largest Full Gospel camp. Life seemed miraculous then, and I dared to believe anything could happen. With this new job, I was beginning to believe that maybe good things were going to come my way.

Maybe the skies were ready to clear up once and for all. Maybe.

24

Best Job Ever

The first day of school came, and I was excited to meet the young people in my class. I stayed a few extra minutes in my meditation that morning, wondering why God would grant my petition to work with hurting youth. Perhaps it had something to do with the fact that if I had the same help growing up, I might not have had to deal with everything I had.

That first day, I could never have anticipated how my studies in mental health would be an advantage and how my experience at summer camp had prepared me for this position. All the pieces of the jigsaw puzzle seemed to fall into place. I could finally see the path I thought I had lost so long ago.

I knew I had been called to work with young people when I was younger. The call from God that I had heard and understood from my youth also referred to my current role at the school. I hadn't understood this until now. I could see all the hurt in the students and could relate to their pain perfectly. It made me feel I had extra potential since I had to grow through a similar path to find myself.

I knew my first day would be challenging, and of course, the students didn't like my supervisor or me. Although he had been in the teaching system for about eight years now, this was his first year in the program. The students were defiant, and a few could not even read because of other disabilities, causing even more behavioral issues. It was like Cameron and Cindy all over again, but I was better armed this time.

Some students were brilliant but had ended up in this program because of questionable outside influences. Many came from single-parent homes or were being raised by a grandparent. Another common factor was parental drug or alcohol abuse, which affected how the students acted at school. Some students with the most severe behavior did not have mothers consistently in their life or had stepdads with abusive tendencies. Some of my students used or sold drugs, and a few even did both. They were a mess and going through things they didn't deserve.

From my own life experiences, I knew the signs well, and it was easy for me to figure out what my students were doing. Maneuvering my way into their softest spots was quite a task, but the rest became easy once I got the hang of it. When I confronted them, they responded with respect. One student, Manuel, once told me, "I wish you were my mother."

"Why would you say that, Manuel?" I asked, concerned that a child as young as he was thought about that.

"No one else cares about me, Miss." He answered, his voice striking a chord in me. I wondered if it was how Cindy had felt when I had to give Cameron my undivided attention. I, myself, had certainly felt this way with my own mother growing up.

"I would adopt you in a moment," I replied, smiling and patting him on the head.

I told my husband about my students all the time and expressed how I wished I could adopt this student. Now and then, Matthew was a voice of reason, despite his many flaws and inadequacies. This was one of those times.

"You can't just adopt everyone," he said as he fought between listening to me and embracing the warm arms of sleep. "You have children of your own. How would you take care of all of them?"

In my heart, I knew he was right. There was no way. I lacked the capacity for five children alongside a demanding job. But as a mother, I couldn't help having maternal feelings toward my students.

These students were selected for the program because their behavior affected the learning of the general student population. Their behavior impeded the learning of other students to such a severe degree that they had to be self-contained or monitored every fifteen minutes of the school day. I was that monitor. My students were always getting into fights, usually at war with one another, and sometimes even taking a swing at the principal. I was expected to bring that to the barest minimum.

Being a teacher's aide was not easy. Sometimes I felt I wasn't making a difference in the lives of these students. Some teachers had a hard time working with these boys. I could manage them, but the students with behavioral issues were in a different ball game. They were like predators where only the strong could survive. They attacked physically and verbally. Even when they said or did nothing, their inactions were closely monitored.

During my pregnancy, their constant fights often took a toll on me. I often asked the Lord to lead me about these boys. Why did He allow me to get a job here? How should I deal with them? I thought about this every day until an answer began to ring over and over in my head.

"Just love them and pray always for them."

So that's what I began to do; love them. I prayed for the boys every morning and talked to them as if I were their mother. Their response to me was impressive. They paid attention to everything I said and never failed to apologize when I called them out on their B.S. At work, I believed things were getting better.

But at home, things had become volatile and dangerous. When I first met my husband, he had promised me the world, but now, all he gave me was a headache. I married someone just like my stepfather; Matthew had taken control of my home. He was unable to keep a job and was stubborn and irrational. Each time Matthew didn't get his way, he would make us pay, going into fits of rage, destroying our home, and smashing everything he knew could shatter into pieces, especially gifts from my mother and sister. Matthew was particularly resentful of them, probably because he didn't particularly feel the same about them. Physical abuse was all too common at our place, even during my pregnancy. Matthew didn't see me when I hurt, as all he cared about was making himself heard. The children meant nothing to him, and all of Cindy's affection was ignored.

Finally, the time came for my last baby to arrive. When it happened, I was so thankful she was healthy and normal. Although six weeks was the allotted time for maternity leave at the school I worked at, I took just two weeks. Besides, where would we get money to keep the house running if I stayed longer at home without going to work? Matthew didn't have a job. Luckily, that meant he could keep both babies while I worked. However, when I was home at night, I woke up every two hours to feed the new baby and woke again a few hours later to go to work. It took a toll on me, but I knew I could handle it perfectly.

My supervisor and principals believed I was a saint. They thought that it was my love for the boys which made me so keen to resume work. However, it helped that I missed my boys. The program was interesting that way; there were only boys in my class, so that was why I called them my boys.

And while I did miss the boys at school, I knew that my eagerness to return to work had less to do with the boys and more with my poor financial situation at home. If I had stayed home for the whole six weeks, there was no way we would survive it. Getting help from anyone was out of the picture.

When I returned, the boys were excited to see me. They wanted to see pictures; they wanted to know about the baby. Their happiness was so infectious, but I noticed that Manuel was not happy. It was apparent with his countenance. I recognized it as worry that Manuel thought the new baby would cause me to overlook him. My children looked at me this way each time I brought home a new sibling. It was something they couldn't help but show.

I also understood this look because of an experience I had as a teenager. During those years, my youth pastors were the world to me, and because I didn't have a father, Pastor John was like a surrogate dad. When they had their first baby, I was sad because I thought they could never love me as much as they did before the baby's arrival. So, I knew what Manuel was going through, I just wasn't sure how to handle it.

"Miss," Manual said to me with bleary eyes, "We're your kids too, right, Miss?"

The classroom froze, and everyone waited for my answer in absolute silence. At that moment, it dawned upon me that Manuel wasn't the only one unsure whether my new baby would change how I treated the class.

I didn't know how to answer, so I motioned for them to return to their desks. I used those few minutes to think of something reassuring to say, as communicating correctly was essential to their psychological health.

Finally, I stood before the class and said, "Yes, I have kids at home, but I care about each of you as well. You are more than just students to me. I pray for you every day. If it were left to me, I would adopt you all in the blink of an eye. I would make sure you got through college. I know each of you can make it, and I want to make sure that you do," I took a deep breath before adding, "So yes, you are my kids, and I love each of you. Even you, Ernie."

"Stop, Miss," Ernie said, blushing.

I wasn't lying. I really did love the boys. These were my children, all of them. I wanted them to make it through the school year, and more importantly, I wanted them to make it in life, just as I wished for my biological kids.

My first day back went well, but home was a different story. My husband was in one of his moods, and we had to steer clear each time that happened. Apparently, he did not precisely have a ball taking care of the kids. It is the same with all men, I think. As women, we are told from the beginning of time that a woman's job is to take care of her kids. Somehow, women seem to do so much work and still barely get any recognition for it, especially from their partners. Our men seem to think that it's so easy staying at home, doing the dishes, doing the laundry, making food, looking after the kids, and the list goes on and on. They seem to think that just because a woman is staying at home means she does not have to do much, or the work she does is effortless. It's only when you turn the tables on them and ask them to fill up just half of your shoes by taking care of the kids that they begin to crumble under pressure.

Matthew was going through something similar.

I did not know what to do or say to him to make him feel better about things. All I could think of was just to pray and ask the Lord to show me his heart again. It seemed to make things clearer to me. I wanted a family with him, but I did not want my children to go through any more craziness. They had gone through so much already, at such young, tender ages.

That night I cried out in repentance for all my disobedience. I cried for the Lord to show me his heart, and I swore that I would listen to what He told me this time. I prayed for the strength and willingness to listen, as I knew that even though I wanted to, I still needed help from God.

25

I Saw the Sign

The same night when I had cried so hard and prayed to God, begging him to show me what to do with my husband, Matthew threw a huge fit. This time, it reminded me of a toddler not getting his way. He made so much noise, stamping his feet all over the living room. He reminded me of four-year-old Cameron when I tried to reduce his sugar intake by taking away candy he found.

It was as awful as all his previous fits. Matthew would disappear somewhere as a habit after having these fits of anger and rage. Then he would come back, calm and incredibly apologetic, pretending not to remember what he had done. I would end up forgiving all the hurtful poison he had spewed when he was consumed by anger because I could not throw out my husband and the father of two of my children, even though I was greatly tempted to do that.

I would tell myself that we were all damaged and bruised, giving excuses for his actions. I don't know how often I told myself that we are still beautiful despite the damage. It became like a lullaby to me each time Matthew had his outbursts. I would go on to justify his actions with questions like, "So, what if Matthew had problems? Did I not have problems of my own?" I remember constantly telling myself that if I continued judging so harshly all the men that came into my life, then my kids and I would never have a shot at a decent life. It was the image I had cooked up in my head, what I chose to live with.

Every time Matthew showed me his worst side, I would end up forgiving him. Then, there would be a short period of peace until he started the cycle again with another fit of drunken rage. However, this time, Matthew's rage fit began to look a little different. Something inside me told me that this was my sign from God, the sign I had previously prayed for. I took action immediately.

I called Bay Area Turning Point because nowhere else came to my mind. I wasn't sure how I would have a different life than this one, and I wasn't even sure if it was ever possible. I had made Matthew leave before, but we both knew he would always return. I couldn't afford childcare and a place to live on my small salary. He knew this, of course, and it left me feeling trapped and scared. I asked God to give me the strength I needed because if this burden was left all on me, I wasn't sure how long I would last.

I swore that I would never settle again. I promised that I would live a life of purity and devotion to Him once I left Matthew. It was no longer worth cheating on God, ignoring all the promises He had made me. I meant everything I said to God that day and still do today.

I had already talked to the shelter but had to wait until it was safe to leave because I had never left Matthew before. It had always been him leaving and then returning. The staff there helped me devise a plan to ensure he wouldn't suspect anything until we were safely out. I stocked the refrigerator with his favorite beer and ensured his pockets were full of our family's money. Then I waited because I knew I was not going to get out of the house with his children while he was around, and I could never leave the house without them. So, I prepared myself to endure whatever was going to happen that night because once it was over, he would leave, and then we could too.

There were no angry outbursts that night, but he did sneak away. And so did we.

I took one day off after we made our escape to settle in, then I went back to work. On getting to the school where I worked, I found a message on my cell phone from the superintendent of human resources, Mr. Mennis. He was wondering why I was working for the district. He hired so many people that he must not have remembered that we had already spoken before, and at great length, when I was applying to be a substitute teacher.

When I returned his phone call, he had plenty to say about my background check. He told me that he was not sure why I had been allowed to work in the school district and that we needed to have a meeting. I again assured him that I was sorry for my mistakes and reminded him that one of the arrests was due to mistaken identity. After I explained this, pleading that I could not be fired for things I had already disclosed, Mr. Mennis recommended that I get these offenses expunged from my record. I wondered why he was bringing it up again after all this time. I thought I had gotten past that already.

I felt like my whole existence was caving in on me in a single instant. Was I going to lose my job? I loved this job, even though the pay was low because I knew I belonged there, and the students needed me. When I asked Mr. Mennis when he would like me to come in for a meeting, he told me we had just had the meeting. He apparently had said everything he felt needed to be said and called my supervisors to make them aware of my background check. After my sudden separation from Matthew, this felt too much for me to handle. I could feel the crashing waves threatening to pull me under the sea, and there was no lifejacket available to keep me afloat.

Mr. Carnes went down to the administration building and fought for me. His efforts, combined with the fact that I had fully disclosed all of my prior grievances, prevented the district from firing me. I did find out, however, that my husband's cousin's girlfriend, Beth, was the one who had alerted the school. She wanted me fired because her son went to the same school where I worked, not that any of that was my doing. She believed I had been telling the school staff all kinds of rumors about her, and Beth didn't want any of her dirty laundry being revealed to strangers. She hated being the center of negative attention.

But nothing could be further from the truth. I had never said anything about Beth to the staff, nor had the thought ever crossed my mind to do so. I always considered her family and I would never have violated her trust. Even after she led a campaign to have me removed from the job that I loved, I never told anyone about her addictions. The irony is that one year later, she was arrested for cocaine possession, and all of her problems were out in the open. I did not find pleasure in that, as I worried more about her children, who had to suffer because of her addiction. But it did strengthen my belief in the fact that God is just in all His ways.

I have learned not to block the Lord's work in someone else's life and to allow God to fight my battles. These are not easy aspirations, as humans find it difficult to surrender and be vulnerable to any being. We think we can solve everyone's problems, heading straight for it without thinking about our weaknesses. And when someone attacks you, it is human instinct to want to defend yourself. But the Bible tells us to agree with our adversaries, and that's what I did.

I had heard through the grapevine that there were rumors that I would be fired. I went to my supervisors, explained what had happened in my younger years, and assured them that it was all in the past. At that time, it had been ten years since I was arrested for public lewdness. I knew I was the poster child for being young and stupid, but I had changed. I had only faulted Beth for preventing me from providing for my family. God took care of the rest.

I called my mother, who was a police officer. She said she would help me pay to have my record expunged, so I called the district attorney's office. The assistant district attorney I spoke to was very helpful. He set me up with the proper paperwork and explained everything I would need to do in detail. It took about six months of endless paperwork, calls, and waiting before my record was cleared of the charge of prostitution. I was never a prostitute! Just a dancer. It made me angry that people still chose to mix up both occupations, probably because of their nature and the commonality in the places where both are exhibited. I was glad that was all gone.

Now, I needed to figure out what to do with the public lewdness charge. Even with just that on my record, I felt so unworthy of being allowed to work in public education. I knew my faults, and I was scared that others would think I was a piece of three-week-old trash, coupled with the fact that I had to engage the mind of minors every day. What would their parents think if they found out? There was no amount of explanation I could give to a plethora of angry parents clamoring for a change in staff.

Working in education made me feel so wonderful, even if I was just an aide. The only bad part about it was that I had to do it amongst intelligent people, and it made me feel a little unworthy, even if I wanted to fit in so badly with my coworkers. But I never gave the impression that I thought I was better than my students or coworkers. For the first time in my life, I acted humble because I wanted to be humble. I was simply grateful for my children and my job. Every other ambition that people struggled for in life - fame, wealth, presence, recognition- failed to mean anything to me as long as I had my family and peace of mind with me.

Our program became very successful during that year, and my supervisors and the principals respected me. When there were problems with my class, they asked my opinion about it. Not only did they ask my opinion, but they also actually listened to me, implementing all the ideas I had offered. This was a new experience, as no one had valued my thoughts before. There had been very few times in my life where I had felt important, and this was one of them. It was all for the right reasons this time, not because I was undergoing withdrawal from drugs or because of some pity resulting from the birth of my first child. This was me being the best version of myself and getting appreciated for it.

This was the best job I had ever had, and it made me decide to go back to college and get my teaching degree. My supervisor had received a promotion to assume the position of principal at another campus, and the head of my school wanted me to take over. But the district said I would first need to have a degree. Well, that was okay with me. I was hoping it would only take a couple of years. I was so proud that the heads of my school thought I would be an excellent person to lead a classroom. My life felt amazing.

I started taking classes at the College of Biblical Studies to finish my degree. This was a good arrangement for me as I would get to study the Bible and, in return, receive an accredited degree in counseling that I could use to teach. I knew I was in accordance with the perfect will of God, and there was comfort in that.

26

The Birth of Some New Ideas

Summer came, and I missed work greatly. There was no longer the worries and apprehension I woke up with every morning; my concern about Adrian, who was always sulking at the back of the class, or Scott, who hid his fear behind drugs. They were all absent, making me feel like something was missing. I looked forward to seeing my boys at the beginning of the next school year. However, I thought I should make the most of this time and focus on other aspects of my life.

Like, my inadequate parenting skills, for example.

I bought parenting books, started reading, and studied the word of God concerning parenting and children. I put my two older children in counseling and began to get involved with educational and faith-based groups that were offered at the shelter. I attended assertiveness, Bible studies, classes on good parenting, and church services. Let's call it a deep-seated desire to want to influence the little world around me positively.

My children were thrilled to be the top priority in my life, laughing and smiling easily at the little jokes I said and the funny things that happened around the house. I couldn't remember the last time that had happened. I spent more time just talking to them, wanting to know how they thought and what they liked. It was something I wasn't conversant with, with my constant search for a job and trying to prove myself at my place of work. This summer break taught me that my children had many different thoughts and opinions. I learned more about their likes and dislikes. One of their dislikes was my meatloaf, but it was nice to see that they ate it anyway.

Even though some of my past decisions had caused so much pain and heartache, the recent ones were shaping my way of thinking, how my children behaved, and the light in which they saw me. I had spent so much time trying to give them the best that I might have forgotten about giving them the thing they wanted most; me. It was obvious that they desired to spend time with me above all else. Oh wait, I was kidding. They also wanted a lot of pizza, but you get the picture. They definitely wanted more time with me.

I had spent my childhood feeling lonely, convinced that I had no one that I could count on, always blaming my family for never being there. Somehow, I had ended up unconsciously doing the same to my kids. It was like it was written in the stars that I would fail hard at everything I tried to embark on; jobs, marriage, adulting, children…but it was high time I changed that narrative. Despite trying hard to prevent this from happening, it still did. This realization broke my heart. But deep down, I knew that only God could fix this.

At the age of 30, I vowed to take it no more! No more sleeping around, putting anything before my Lord, or putting any human person before my children. No more me, just Him. It was finally time to get it right.

During that summer, I ran into a couple of my students at the mall and one time in the public library along the corner of the shelter. They assured me they were behaving correctly and were looking forward to seeing me again at school. I had hoped to run into Manuel, but I never did. Manuel was due to get off probation soon, and I feared he would have to move back in with his father, a man with many issues of his own. Unless Manuel got away from such a strong negative influence, I worried that he would never get very far, because he would only get dragged into problems and habits that he hadn't bargained for.

During probation, Manuel was sentenced to live with his grandmother, a law-abiding citizen. The judge knew he needed some form of stability to grow and improve. But now that that was almost over, there was also the presence of Manuel's brother, who also tended to lead him into trouble. His brother was more likely to hang around with their father, which significantly threatened Manuel's mental health. I prayed for Manuel daily, asking God to do something about his impending situation.

Summer passed, and with it came the end of the school break. The first day of school approached, but there was no sign of Manuel, his head bobbing around the hallway searching for me. I assumed it was probably an illness or something of that nature, as I had heard the flu was prevalent then. The second day came, but Manuel still wasn't there. I could feel something was wrong. My sixth sense was trying to tell me something.

I asked my supervisor about Manuel, and we found out he had been arrested after getting released from probation. His older brother had talked him into breaking into a house, and the police were alerted by an informant. Manuel was caught red-handed at the scene of the crime. After learning this news, I went to the bathroom and poured my eyes out. It was the worst possible news. Maybe I should have tried to make contact with my students during the summer. I should have tried to help his grandmother, brought food, and done something to stay involved. Was I wrong to have focused solely on self-development and parental grooming?

Over the next few months, I couldn't stop thinking about Manuel. However, life and time are cruel and wait for nobody. The year flew by, and we had to go on without him. Our program was a success, as the students were staying out of trouble, and my supervisor wasted no time getting everyone conversant with the fact that I was a big reason for that. The program's success even played a part in his promotion to principal. Also, I was doing well in my college classes, and I was eager to complete my degree.

Sometime during the summer, I took Matthew back, understanding that I couldn't possibly take care of 4 children without him. But before I could say Jack Robinson, my husband began doing his disappearing acts all over again, which were starting to get old. I even had to place a missing persons' report once because he was gone for two weeks, and I figured he was dead this time. But that would have been an easy way out of my mistake.

I needed mental support. I was raising a family, a husband, and the children at my job. I longed for the support I had once received from the Esther group at church because since it broke up, I felt really alone. With everything I had accomplished, there was still some emptiness inside me. It mirrored the one I felt when I thought I needed a man in my life, but now, I knew better. I knew better than to believe that some man would make me feel whole. I was not naïve anymore.

One night during my last year in college, I had a dream that seemed so vivid and natural. In the dream, I had started a support group at my church that went nationwide. It was great, just like Esther's group, but it focused more on outreach. I woke up with a clear and definitive message: I was going to restart the single moms' group.

The following Sunday after church, I went to Pastor Jeanna and asked her if I could restart the single moms' group. She said, "Tyra, I think that is a wonderful idea, but I want you to ask Jennifer to help."

Jennifer had stepped in to help the Esther group when Lynn had first resigned. I was hoping she would be willing to help because she had her own house and lived close to the church, while I lived 25 miles away in an apartment. Jennifer would be an incredible asset in putting me through the ropes of starting the group and helping me draw up a schedule and all the other tasks that needed to be done. I called her up to invite her to help, and Jennifer was so excited.

"Actually," she said, "starting the single mom's group has been on my heart for a while now. I just wasn't sure when to get it going."

Jennifer was happy that I had heard from God, and her enthusiasm made me confident that this was what He had intended. We discussed the ins and outs of the group and agreed that the name Esther did not accurately describe our group in its entirety. Even though I was married, I was raising my children alone, which was something to be considered in creating a name, as many other women were like that too.

"We have mothers raising children alone," Jennifer said, angling her head and swirling the ball pen held firmly in her right hand.

"That's it!" I almost jumped from the sudden realization. "Mothers Raising Children Alone! We can use the acronym MRCA."

And this is how MRCA came into being. Our support group had mothers who were divorced, mothers whose husbands were in jail, and even grandmothers. For whatever reason, they were raising children alone and needed a way to vent. The group was their solace and opportunity to get encouragement from people in the same situations.

Jennifer and I had a grand vision of what we wanted for the group. I saw it as a prominent organization where both women and men could benefit from the support of one another. I wanted our group to meet once a month and talk about things we had to overcome as single parents, introducing strategies on how to stay faithful to God and committed to our children. I wanted to document effective methods for choosing a suitable mate and being involved in the lives of other parents. Regardless of how they ended up raising their children alone, group members would bring a new and fresh perspective to the challenge of parenting. I needed this group, and the group needed me. It was a refreshing development.

During the time that MRCA was getting started, my school was going through some specific changes. One of the teachers came to work intoxicated and was subsequently fired. Rumors circulated that she had taken part in an inappropriate relationship with a former student, and the school had gotten wind of it after she tried to call it off. The student was making a whole lot of noise about it. The teacher's replacement was overwhelmed by the job and quit after just a few months, giving the school only 15 minutes prior notice. The school was in distress over what to do.

Knowing I had already passed my content test in special education but had not graduated yet, I never considered that there was a possibility of my getting a promotion. It never even occurred to me. But on a particular day during lunch hours, the members of the human resource department of the school pulled me into a surprise meeting and informed me that I would be teaching English language arts for the remainder of the year.

The administration said my success with the adaptive behavior program showed that I was ready for my own classroom. They told me there were some substantial behavior problems in this particular classroom, but due to my experience in the other program, they were confident that I could handle it. I would not be paid a regular teacher's salary but would gain the knowledge I needed to be hired as a teacher for next fall.

My elation superseded my need for financial buoyancy at that moment. The Lord had counted me among the faithful again, presenting me another opportunity to shine. Even though I wasn't officially considered the teacher on record, I was proud to switch from being an aide to a regular classroom teacher. It felt like I had just been included in a sacred sorority.

27

To New Beginnings

February 2nd was my first day as a new teacher, and it was the beginning of an eventful journey. The students were purposely rotten, exhibiting acts of defiance and disobedience. Students would turn their papers in written in Spanish just for fun, and I would then put down my comments in Spanish, instructing them to rewrite in English. I gave out many detentions in the first week, as cautions and warnings weren't enough to get them to behave appropriately. They called me prejudiced and thought that I didn't like Mexicans. I had learned from working in the behavior and the shelters that waging a power struggle with people you have no control over would only have you looking like a fool in the end.

On the first working day of the following week, I made sure I had a wedding picture along with pictures of my kids sitting on my desk. So, the next time I was called prejudiced, I would turn around the picture of my

Hispanic husband and I on our wedding day. After that subtle act, I earned some level of respect from some of the students. The other students were shocked when they found I understood the street slang. Among them, it was said, "Don't mess with Ms. Wilson. She is a gangster."

I was apprehending the students who cheated in examinations easily, but I don't think I was doing anything particularly extraordinary that no other teacher on this planet could. Didn't they understand we were all young at a point in our lives? Did these teenagers think that all their teachers were born disciplined? It was easier to understand the students while armed with the knowledge of my ways when I was still in school.

Nothing teaches us better than our own mistakes. And in my thirty years of life, I had made several. Interestingly, every mistake I made was more significant than the former, and each new one hurt me more than the last. Each of those mistakes taught a lesson greater than the previous. It was like a gradient, and I, an observer.

When they knew I wasn't going anywhere, my students finally began to trust me, accepting the notion I had come with. I heard their stories and I listened, as I understood that kids loved to be heard and acknowledged. Many said that I was not like the other teachers. I instilled the belief in my students that anyone could attend college, and they embraced it. I had relatable guest speakers come in and talk about their struggles as they worked on college degrees. I wanted my students to believe that anyone could finish high school, attend college, and graduate with flying colors. They just had to find the college which was right for them.

If you work in education, you would be conversant with the fact that the kids coming to your class may be going through a lot of difficulties at home and may be leading confusing lives. They are probably surrounded by people who only know how to criticize them and nothing else. The best you could do is to offer hope and encouragement, as your teaching method should build and not break them down.

Each student in your class has potential, and the teacher is mandated to assist them in making the best use of it. I narrated my story to them, hoping it would be an inspiration to them. Obviously, I did not tell them everything about my past, but I didn't hide the fact that I had a very rough start. If I could rise from the ashes, so could they.

At the end of the school year, my students had an 80 percent pass rate on the statewide test. This was impressive, considering I was the third teacher they'd had that year. They had, in all seven periods, A's and B's. Some even received commendations for their test scores, as their performance level was astounding. I felt so blessed.

But the end of the school year brought another bout of anxiety about my employment for the following year. I worried that I wouldn't find a job as a certified teacher, despite the assurances given my experience in the past year. I was due to graduate in three months, and I still wondered if my background would continue to count against me. Although my record was expunged of some offenses, it was still far from perfect.

Just as I did when I had wanted to be an aide, I sent a resume to every school in my district. Since I only received a couple of calls then, I assumed it would be the same when I applied to be a teacher. But I was wrong. I took a Thursday off to send my resumes and cover sheets to every school in our district, delivering 11 of them physically and sending the rest via mail. In just a couple of years, our district had grown to 77 schools, thus accounting for the large number of my resumes that went out. I had only gotten a few calls when I applied to be a paraprofessional. So, I expected to receive only a few phone calls now.

By the time I got home from hand delivering the 11 resumes, five messages were already waiting for me on my cellphone. Over the next two days, I received so many phone calls. It was crazy! It escalated when they discovered I had adaptive behavior experience, as principals began to offer me jobs over the phone. Before receiving the massive number of phone calls, I had already made a verbal commitment to the first school, believing it would be my only offer.

My phone rang endlessly for hours. I tried to explain to one particular principal that I had already made a verbal commitment to another school, but she couldn't care less. She asked, "Don't you even want to come to check it out?"

"Ma'am," I wondered why they weren't getting it. "I have already made a verbal commitment to another principal. I can't go back on my words."

"But you haven't signed a contract, right?" The principal was relentless, and I liked that about her.

"Ma'am, I am really flattered, but I have to go with integrity on this one." I almost succumbed to the desire to hang up on this woman, as her persistence was choking. Honestly, I was flattered that someone wanted me.

The phone calls did not stop even after informing each of them that I already had a secured job offer. It got so bad that I had to unplug the phone. I was also tired of telling people I had already found a teaching position but couldn't sign a contract until I graduated in two months. They all wanted to get me hooked down before then.

In August 2007, I graduated from college and began teaching students with autism. Once again, the Lord had shown me favor with the students as well as my supervisors. My program was blessed, and my students were learning more than I could have imagined. My first year as a certified teacher was terrific, and my prior experience with students made it all the more enjoyable. I prayed daily for my students as well as my own children.

At home, my children and I began to have weekly Bible studies and we shared what God had done for us that week. Cameron and Cindy were growing in grace and favor. They were no longer the wild children they used to be, with recurring psychological traumas. Also, in 2007, we discovered that God had blessed Cindy with a beautiful singing voice and hearing her sing around the house made my heart swell with pride. When I see what God has done for our family, joy fills my heart.

28

The Second-Best Year Ever

In 2009, my year was blessed. It was when I received a 100 percent pass rate for my student's statewide assessment. Everyone but me was shocked, as I understood it was either that or nothing. I now understand that God can do anything. How, then, could I record anything less than success? It was also this year that one of my students with autism was reevaluated. The outcome of his revaluation was that he was no longer autistic. You might question the possibility of this happening, as I sometimes did.

Maybe it can all be attributed to my sleepless nights, down on my knees, praying for divine healing for each of my students. The intriguing thing is that I have more students up next year for reevaluation, and they will assuredly find the same thing with them. I won't get to see it, though, because I received a promotion. I am no longer a teacher but a Behavioral Specialist for a new district.

In February 2009, Mothers Raising Children Alone was incorporated and is now operating as a non-profit organization. Our mission is to bring college education into the homes of single parents. Whether it is a guardian or child, we want to be able to get them through college.

I finally filed for divorce from Matthew in March. The disappearing acts alone told me I had a biblical reason to get away from him. Although I grieved because I knew God's stand where divorce is concerned, I knew it was a decision that had to be made. After going through so much pain and misery, while providing many chances to work out our differences but never detecting willingness on his part, I knew that parting ways was the only option.

I now place my whole trust in God, more invested in fostering a relationship with Him. In May, I was able to be a spokesperson for an event hosted by Bay Area Turning Point. There, I spoke about everything they had done for me, including paying for my teaching certificate. My whole family is experiencing the beauty and blessings of God.

I finally decided it was time to do something about that public lewdness issue. My life had finally turned around completely, and I could not afford to have my background ruin my promising career. So, I filed paperwork for a Full Pardon from the State. This would enable me to remove the charge of public lewdness from my police record and further facilitate my employability status. After a few months, I received a letter in the mail from the Texas Board of Pardons and Parole, recommending me for a Full Pardon. Although the governor of Texas still has to append his signature on the papers, giving his legal consent, I am nevertheless going to walk in faith, hoping he does provide me with one. It was a big deal for the board to recommend me because hundreds of people apply yearly, and very few make it to the point I reached.

I feel honored and incredibly blessed. Like Hester Prynne, the scarlet letter on my chest no longer stood for adulteress, fornicator, harlot, or anything of that nature. Like Hester, it stood for Able. God was able to complete in me everything He had started, despite my selfish will and desires constantly getting in the way. Now, I would be able to do everything He called me to do. The burning mess of my former life sparked flames of a new destiny. I rose out of the fire like a Phoenix.

29

Life Anew

My life was back on track in all the ways that seemed to matter most. Now I just had to focus on my education and see what positive results I could yield from it. My passion for teaching, springing from the fluidity of the course of my life, was more vital than ever, and I was ready to change lives in every way that I could. It was all I wanted; being in the classroom and helping students learn and assimilate faster. I taught for a while, loving every minute of it. But I could not deny the fact that I wasn't satisfied; that there was a yearning in me to go further.

I needed more.

I felt I could have more impact if I helped the most troubled students, the ones other learning instructors struggle to help. Subsequently, I made a very bold move, applying for a job as a behavioral specialist at Cypress Park school. This meant working in the classroom with severely disadvantaged students in one way or another, but it was what I wanted to do. And it was where I could make my mark.

After my first day on the job, my nerves melted when I saw how well I had settled into the role. A week later, the seams were totally invisible, and all the cracks were patched. I was having tremendous success after only a month, and everything was going well. It was unbelievable being paid for something I loved. More demanding was the fact that my students all had some emotional disturbances that required my assistance to help them stay focused on learning. Every day was a challenge and an accompanying recorded success.

But beyond that, I had set my sights even higher than working in the classroom; I wanted to become the district's behavioral specialist at the elementary school level. I knew if I could land the position, I would spend my days traveling around the district, performing interventions, and helping the specially challenged kids. The trajectory was set, and my life was on course to reach that ultimate dream.

Over the first two years, I had a mix of children with severe autism and behavioral concerns, and I handled them almost perfectly, making them seem like every other child at school. My supervisors were impressed with my work, remarking that it seemed I had a gut instinct about what the students needed. Perhaps, it was a sixth sense. I even worked with my students' families in school, and at home, identifying issues in the family's dynamic that might be addressed to help the student integrate better educationally. I appreciated how much they trusted me to guide them so that their students would fare better. There I was, making the difference I had always dreamed of.

When students were suspended on account of their actions, they came to me to help with their Disciplinary Alternative Education Program (DAEP) to help improve their behavior. My successes in education were piling up, and although there were hurdles, I loved my work. Cypress Park was amazed, and my supervisors loved it.

But my successes weren't limited to work.

My church was organizing outreach to women working in strip clubs, and since I had some experience in that area, I felt it was incumbent on me to participate. I admit that, at first, I was hesitant. I was apparently battling my demons from the life I once lived. My transition from that life felt fresh from that moment of encounter, even though quite some time had passed. There is no way to tell how long it can take before your past finally stays in the past. Even with a bachelor's degree attached to my portfolio and a respectable new job, I was haunted by my yesterdays. Walking through those doors into the strip club again took me back to the shame and the pain of those moments with my top off, dancing on top of a table, and shouting at the top of my lungs. But I couldn't turn my back on those women. I knew what it meant to feel like that form of life was the only way to support themselves. I knew the tragic stories that drove women to the clubs. It was once my story as well, and I knew I had to go back and share my story.

After I started the outreach, I went home, heavy-laden with my concern for the many women trapped by that lifestyle. Uneasy and wanting to do something about it, I started writing my story. I wrote out all my pain, shame, and struggles to escape a life that robbed me of dignity and purpose. I wrote for unending hours until my fingers hurt, then went numb. Even after that, I wrote some more.

Initially, I thought that my writings would be done in a pamphlet, but there was too much to tell to contain in the pages of a tiny publication. I needed to write a book. As shocking as that sounded to me, I dove right in. It was one thing I learned about having a glimpse of a dream or an idea. The moment it is not acted upon, it disappears without a trace, like it was never there to begin with.

When the book was completed, I surveyed my work and breathed a sigh of relief. I had done it and I was proud of every word. It was a message walking arm-in-arm with redemption, worthy of any publisher.

So began the quest to get my work published. I submitted excerpts of the manuscript to several publishers, anticipating responses. When I heard back from one of the publishers, I could not contain my joy. The company wanted to see more pages of the manuscript with the intention of considering it for publication. I was on pins and needles for months after obliging their request, waiting for their response. Just when I thought they might have lost interest in reading more pages, I received a contract in the mail to publish the story. I screamed out my excitement as I read it off the many papers. My work had been validated, but it was more than that. My triumph over my old life had been authenticated. My story was as powerful as I thought, and the publisher believed that others would want to read it.

Suddenly, as intensely as it had come, my joy faded into fear. I was putting my story out there for the world to see, suddenly making me feel vulnerable and exposed. It meant everyone would know who I was and what I had done at one point in my life, something I had tried to keep other people's noses out of. I couldn't predict how the officials at Cypress School would react, and it was worse thinking about my students' parents. I was terrified and decided it was probably best to publish under a pseudonym. I chose my middle name, and the name of the author boldly written on the cover of my book was "Deanna Wilson."

My expectations remained modest, as I felt it was enough to be acknowledged by the publisher. I was not expecting massive sales. But surprisingly, the popularity of the book grew far faster than I had expected. Soon, people were calling me about it, asking questions about how I had lived, and demanding interviews. Then Barnes and Noble in Pasadena, Texas, offered me the opportunity to have a book signing. It was far enough away from home that I was sure the people of the small town of Cypress Springs would not find out about it. But a reporter caught wind of the story and showed up with a camera, covering the entire event. The story made its way into the papers, and a thousand outlets picked up the story and ran it in their documentaries. I had people calling me from everywhere, and my face was plastered on the paper's front page.

A television newscast, Fox 26, picked up the story and asked to do a profile piece on it. They came to my home for the interview and aired it live on their network. The interview was touching, as I got a chance to share the turning point in my life. I explained that this pivotal moment in my journey away from stripping occurred when I was in Pasadena in a crisis pregnancy center. There, I met a wonderful lady named Peggy while I was homeless and pregnant, desperate for answers as to where my life was going. She drove me to a maternity home in Wichita Falls, Texas. She, along with the people there, helped me without ever asking for anything in return.

As my book title indicated, I explored God's grace from the strip clubs to the classroom. I honestly thought everyone would appreciate the rags to spiritual riches story I shared because wasn't that what we were all made to believe? But I soon discovered that sharing my Cinderella story would get me cast out of the palace and into the dungeon.

On the day the interview aired, I was bubbling with excitement. I talked about the love and care I received at the pregnancy crisis center and all the wonderful people who had a hand in changing my life for the better. Book sales were soaring. It was huge. Do you know the moment when something so incredibly beautiful abruptly gets thrown back at you? That's how I felt, like I was walking on cloud 9.

I no longer worried that those at my job would discover that I was Deanna Wilson and that my past was checkered. People seemed to be embracing the story and finding strength and inspiration from it, so I figured it would be the same in the school too. Indeed, my job would be proud to have such a high-performing staff member in their ranks, one who had overcome the odds that way.

I could not have been more wrong.

I had shared with my coworkers, alongside everyone I knew, that the story was going to be aired at 10 that evening. The tick of the clock met me in front of the big-screened television, sprawled on the floor with my children, awaiting the news. We were so excited, celebrating my win together as a family. But I was an educator, and I had broken an unwritten rule. I was expected to be a perfect person with the ideal background, so there was no appreciation for a comeback story in my field, no matter how much positive attention it got.

What was worse was the way the story was presented. As the newscaster told the story, the producers added in B-rolls, stock footage that played on the screen as the reporter spoke. The B-rolls they chose was unsavory, showing a dive joint where people had cocaine on the table, with someone snorting it. The next scene was that of a stripper walking around a pole in a club. When the newscaster talked about me being homeless, the B-roll was of a person sleeping in a garbage bag on the street. I sat there with my mouth agape and my heart pounding out of control. Not only was none of that a part of my story, but I was also being portrayed in the most unfavorable light.

"Oh my God," I whispered, staring at my children in shock. "I am in so much trouble."

When I arrived at school the following day, everyone had seen the story and was taken aback. I went in to talk to my boss, who was equally stunned by the coverage.

"How bad is this?" I asked, trying to stand straight with the shreds of dignity I had left.

She shook her head and wore a somber expression. "I don't know," she murmured, touched by my plight. "I don't know. I don't think I can protect you from this."

My heart fell to my ankles at the sound of her despair. This achievement, which should have been a monumental moment commemorating the successful launch of my first book, became traumatic. I left her office carrying the weight of the world on my shoulders, without a clue that it was about to get even heavier.

I received a phone call from the district as I stepped into my office.

"Hello," the representative said without a bit of emotion. "We need to talk about your book and would like you to come in."

When I arrived, they had just one question. "Are you going to continue to do these news stories?"

It was the $64,000 question. Would I abandon my dream to share my life with others and potentially help other women in my situation? Or would I cave to the pressure to be silent, cower, and retreat? I chose the former and replied confidently, ignoring my shaky hands. "Yes, I'm going to go ahead and promote the book."

They said they needed time to discuss the issue and get back to me, but little did I know that the meeting included the entire board of education for the Cypress Park School District. Behind the scenes, my fate was being decided. Naturally, I could feel anger trying to rear its head. After leading a most traumatic life, I had tried to do something positive, but instead, I was being made to pay a terrible price for it. It was clear that I was in big trouble with my district. I placed a call to the reporter and lashed all of my anger at him.

"Hey," he defended, and I could tell he had one of his hands up in the air. "I was just doing my job."

"Yes," I retorted, irritated that he had the nerve to try and justify all that happened. "But I might just lose my job over it."

"Look," he said quietly. "You wrote the book."

30

Fallout

My perfect world was caving in, and I was thrown in the middle. I felt I had to choose between my book and my career. I knew I couldn't just pull the book out; something that I had worked so hard on, dedicating my time, energy, and emotions. My decision was clear. But despite that stance, I was also scared about losing my job and being blackballed. I did a live news story the next day, determined to stand my ground. When the district and the board saw that I was pressing forward with the book, I was called in to meet with the head of human resources and another high-ranking official just beneath the superintendents. As soon as I stepped in, I knew I was in trouble. It wasn't news that when two people from human resources met up with anyone, it was a telling sign that the issue was on the horizon. The duo was rumored to be called "the angels of death." Usually, when they were seen entering the school building, people lost their jobs, which meant heads were about to roll. I was afraid my head was about to roll.

I sat down cautiously, wondering why I should even bother taking my seat when I knew what they were here for. I wished they had just said, "You're fired," and let me leave with a shred of dignity rather than sit there judging me with their shared stares of disappointment and shame.

"Miss Wilson," one of the duo began, calling out the name I was known as at the time. "We know the book was written with the pseudonym of Tyra, but it is not particularly a secret that it was you. We planned for this meeting to go a different way, but the school board met, and one of the members was a huge supporter. She broke down and demanded that we protect you."

I was in shock. Contrary to my fear that I was about to lose my head, they stated that my story inspired most people at the meeting. It was almost unbelievable. I let myself breathe a sigh of relief, exhaling the breath I had been holding as I'd walked down the long hall toward the meeting room. They explained they had gotten so scared by my story because the town had already experienced an enormous scandal. It was the same town where the mother of a cheerleader was tried in court for putting a hit out on her daughter's rival.

"Look," the second person took over, not wanting to waste any more time on the issue. "We want you to continue with all your interviews. But whatever you do, you must never mention this district. It should never come up in the slightest. And always advise our communications person when you have to give an interview. He can ensure that the interviewer's motives are pure and that your story won't be co-opted again. Reporters are skilled at tripping and twisting your words and intent."

I nodded in acknowledgment, shook their hands, and left the meeting, desperate for a quiet place where I could release all of the emotion that had built up. As I cried out my relief in a private area, I thanked God for the blessing, the protection, and the support of that board member who spoke out so passionately in my defense. They must have held so much conviction to be listened to by the remaining board members. When I returned to work, my supervisor, Mary, who hired me and had always been very friendly with me, suddenly hated me because of the story. She was no longer able to tolerate me, making her displeasure very clear.

Once, when I was speaking in a meeting with other behavioral specialists and a licensed school psychologist, Mary told me that my input didn't matter, announcing that I was at the bottom of the barrel. I was shocked by her comments. But I tried to ignore her spiteful opinions, continuing to do an excellent job recording successes with the kids. But her vocal hatred towards me made me anxious, making it difficult for me to even walk in the corridors of the building. I realized that I needed to start seeking employment elsewhere.

But even that was fraught with dangers.

I had watched Mary give other educators harmful recommendations when they wanted to leave. I had also seen teachers' aides who were ready to become teachers after they finished school but couldn't because of her. She refused to give good suggestions to many of them, her decision based on who she liked and didn't like. I knew that if she did that to people with no reputation issues, I would have a more challenging time getting a recommendation. So, I stayed there for two more years, hoping things would improve enough to leave. But they only got worse, spiraling down the slope.

To make matters worse, they took away my district title. This happened despite the fact that I had a lot of success with the students, achieving what no one else in the district could dare to meet. I was assigned to the most dangerous emotionally disturbed students. They were very violent; children who had no problem hitting me with chairs or throwing out their fists at every opportunity. We often had to restrain them from hurting themselves or others. All the more prominent school districts had programs where kids were protected, but no matter what they did, there was little recourse to the Special Education status.

I knew how to get out of that district, but it took several years. I finished my master's degree and started applying for jobs. During that time, Mary asked me what I would love to do with my master's degree, and I admitted to her that I had always wanted to be a district behavior specialist and was working toward that. I knew it was risky to share that information with her, and as expected, things were awkward at work for some time afterwards. Because of my anxiety and paranoia, I stopped doing interviews to promote the book so that I wouldn't throw more fuel on the fire. I was essentially in breach of contract with my publisher, to which I had agreed to do some promotion. But I didn't want to lose what I had accomplished in education, not after all the effort I had put into it. This constant emotional tug-of-war left me in fear, with frequent panic attacks.

The end-of-the-year evaluation in my third year of education resulted in scores that exceeded expectations; the highest an educator could receive at the time. I had to be very careful and watch my steps, knowing I had to have an excellent recommendation to move from one Texas district to another. I would be required to submit three references, and one had to be from a supervisor. It was something I knew Mary was not going to give me. As a result, my only option was to return to a school district where I had previously been employed. They knew my work ethic and would be happy to have me return. And it certainly didn't need any recommendation from my current supervisor.

A month after I left Cypress, I ran into Mary in the grocery store. I greeted her warmly. She unexpectedly gave me a cordial response, then voiced the question I feared she would ask from the moment I first spotted her. "Why didn't you use me for a reference?"

I thought that was the oddest question ever because of the toxic climate that followed the release of my book and the subsequent interviews. I wanted to answer, "because I knew you weren't going to give me a good one," but I sidestepped the question, asking about her wellbeing instead.

She noticed my evasive attempt and asked, "Where are you working now?"

My paranoia kicked into overdrive, and I could imagine her contacting the school with a copy of my television interview. It was no shocker that I lied and made up a random district that didn't even exist. Thankfully, Texas is so large that there was no way she could know at the time that I was not telling her the truth. I was determined not to let her blackball me. I still had plans to become a district behavior specialist, and she could easily ambush me and throw my goal off course.

31

Family Ties

With my life now back on track, I could pay more attention to my highest priority; my four kids. I had been so stressed and disconnected from all that concerned them that it was necessary to start spending adequate time with them. It was satisfying to know that my ex-husband, as a result of his addiction issues, had gotten into rehab. With him being unavailable most of the time, the kids needed my focus more than ever.

Matthew and I still had feelings for one another, so it was not particularly surprising when he pushed for reconciliation. I wanted to do the right things for the kids, and I thought getting back together with him was a part of it. Foolishly, I thought he had changed and would never do drugs again. So, we ended up getting remarried, with me subsequently taking the big step to change my name to his, something I had not been willing to do during our first marriage.

Things seemed like they were going to be great. We had even bought a house and were settling again as a family, my excitement shining like a bright lantern in an already illuminated place. Along the line, we decided that this was an excellent time to start working toward getting my doctoral degree. I was also doing some speaking engagements now and then, usually for pro-life centers. But public appearances weren't something I often did because I was still afraid that I might go through the same difficulties I had faced at Cypress Park.

In the same pattern that it had occurred throughout the years, on a certain day, my fears were realized. Over the years of his addition, I had grown accustomed to the smell of different drugs, so it was not hard to suspect that my husband was doing drugs again. Crack has its own special odor, and my husband disappeared within a few hours each time I detected it. This pattern gave rise to our first divorce, and I felt us barreling toward a second one, except this time, it was going to be worse than the first.

I turned to his mother for support, but she firmly maintained that her perfect son wasn't up to anything. Her pattern of covering for him despite the alarming amount of evidence and her own actions infuriated me. I felt we should work together since we both had his best interest at heart. But with his addiction growing out of control, I could no longer have him at my house. He had traded our household items for drugs in the past, and I didn't want that to happen again. Once, he even took our car and traded it to crack dealers. This was apparently the continuation of a terrible habit we thought he had let go of. He would go off drugs and remain clean for three months at a stretch, and during that period of sobriety, he was apologetic and sweet, and I always allowed him to weasel his way back into our home. I promised God, I would never let him return if he went back on drugs, but there I was, constantly breaking that promise.

At the same time as my internal drama was getting out of control, I was founding a nonprofit organization called "Mothers Raising Children Alone." I started the program in 2009, and I could say that it was growing exponentially. We had groups all over Houston that fostered the parent connections that single parents desperately needed. We offered parenting classes, playgroups, and other services to the public, also creating an award category for the single mother of the year in an annual grand celebration.

One day, my neighbor across the street approached me, concerned that my husband was always moving in and out of the house like a frequent furniture change. I knew to pay attention to whatever she said because she always seemed exceptionally wise and supportive. She gave me a piece of advice: "If you want to know his true intentions, ask God to show you, his heart."

I knew she was right, as I had been doing this from the moment, I met Matthew. Although he was always so verbal about his love for me and the kids, this evil side drew him into the arms of the streets and drugs. As a result, I wasn't exactly sure of the position of his heart. So, I took my neighbor's advice, praying that God would show me his heart and kept in mind the warning she added to her advice: "Be ready to deal with the repercussions if his heart is not in the right place."

The two youngest of my children were the most vulnerable to the potential loss of their father. They were still so little that they needed to be protected from their parent's pasts, as they had only known a life of privilege. The older two children had seen my ups and downs and all the mess that came with it. They had lived in the shelters with me and saw their father struggle with drugs.

But still, I could not let my children see my husband's downfall or allow one of them to get hurt over something crazy he did in the streets. That afternoon, I went on a walk with the Lord and talked to him about my situation. I voiced my concerns, "God if you would just show me his heart, I will do the right thing. I do not condone divorce, but I will protect my children."

Immediately after my prayers, I walked through our beautiful neighborhood, surrounding myself with the beauty of nature. Abruptly, the fragrance was interrupted by an aroma I knew all too well. It always permeated the atmosphere when Matthew was about to have a relapse on drugs. As expected, he continued his frequent disappearing acts in the days following my prayer. Once, when he left with my car and didn't return, I went searching for him. Ironically, I found him with another woman in the vehicle that solely belonged to his wife. Luckily, I was able to get my car back without much hassle. But the conclusion was clear, written in the clearest font possible; my husband had given his life to drugs, and it was time for me to accept that the only suitable option was to file for a divorce.

Again.

My decision was confirmed when he got arrested. It was like a sign from above, telling me that I could not possibly bring my children up around a man who frequented the county jail. When Matthew was released, he went to live with his mother, having never had a place of his own. I felt confident that the Lord had shown me his heart and led me in the right direction.

Three months later, I fell ill with flu-like symptoms. Matthew called, saying he wanted to come over to care for me and the kids, even offering to cook and clean. It was an appealing offer, but I recognized it as one of his tactics to get back home. And I knew that pushing him out would become challenging to do once he got in. He would say he was sorry again, and I would end up being swayed by how happy I was that he was there with the kids and that I would let him stay. But the Lord had already shown me how insufficient Matthew was and offered me his heart. If I faltered this time, I had no one to blame but myself.

After my refusal, Matthew scored a job with our neighbor and went to Louisiana to work. At this time, I started having vivid dreams that I neither understood their meaning nor just how important they were. But I knew I had a gift in the realm of dreams. My husband was away, making a lot of money working with our neighbor in New Orleans, and I had a dream while he was still there that we were in a house together. It wasn't a great-looking house, with old decor and a damp smell. In the dream, I was in the back room close to a doorway. Matthew would not let me leave that back room. I was trapped there. I had to maneuver past him to see what was happening in the front room. But it felt like it was something he didn't want me to see. All I saw were three people dressed up in nice country clothes. But one of them was a sick-looking woman with a thin face and sunken eyes. I realized then that he didn't want me to know she was there for him.

In the dream, I said, "I want you to go be with your people."

He answered, "No, no, no, no, I want to stay."

I replied, "No, go with your people. There here for you and you need to go"

When I woke, I looked at the clock and saw it was midnight and suddenly had a strong urge to check my bank account. My husband and I still retained a joint account where his checks were deposited, and he had just gotten paid at midnight through a direct deposit. I watched the account for the next couple of hours as the bank account drained by 100 dollars at intervals. Hour by hour, the money was withdrawn. I waited till 5 am before reporting our debit card stolen so that Matthew wouldn't be able to take out any more money.

With everything frozen in that bank account, I could plan how I wanted to move forward. I was entirely done with the whole Matthew saga. Like a physical confirmation of my decision, I picked up my phone and texted him, glancing at the clock. I knew it was still 5 in the morning, but his groggy greeting was not enough to cool my anger. I couldn't care less if he had a busy day and desperately needed to be in bed.

"I'm done," I said with an air of finality, scaring myself with how calm I sounded. "Your crap will be at your mother's house. Do not come back here."

Our marriage ended for the second and last time. All I had to do now was get my car back from him, as he had taken it on one of his aimless pursuits. I could be liable if he traded it to a dope dealer involved in a crime.

My decision left my soon-to-be ex-husband stuck in Louisiana, but I really couldn't care. I was beyond any form of positive emotions towards him. I instructed him to stay away from the kids until he was clean and sober enough to guarantee their safety. With that chapter of my life closed, it was time to resume the pursuit of my doctorate, a task that required exceptional focus and a strict schedule of simultaneously carrying out duties in the single-parent support groups, not to mention taking care of my kids and working. There was little room for drama.

My life was consumed with responsibilities for the next three years, as I worked through all the basic classes on my doctorate and developed a system to ensure my kids were stable. The support groups I had established were thriving, and it was gratifying to see lives being changed. One, in particular, was incredibly heart-warming. She was a young woman named Ashley who had gotten pregnant in her teens. But now, she was a dedicated mom, totally committed to the program. Over time, she became like a family. Once she completed the program, she asked to start her group in East Houston. I felt she was ready. Ashley had a twin sister named Angela, and she always called me Mom. Together, they worked on establishing the group, and both did a fabulous job.

There was also Keyshia, a single mom with a young daughter, who became tightly knit with me as well. Keyshia got married, but her commitment to the group would not allow her to abandon it even after she became a married mother. She continued to support and inspire the other women coming into the program. That was what a family meant. We shared our holidays, especially during Christmas and Thanksgiving, helping young mothers through the most challenging times of life and giving out hundreds of turkeys.

Life was good. But the past remained a haunting reminder. I was still suffering from bouts of anxiety and abrupt concerns that Mary was looking for me, intent on exposing me at the cost of my new job. It felt crazy and unmanageable in light of my responsibilities, but I couldn't help my train of thought. It took years before I realized that I was suffering from post-traumatic stress. I just knew I didn't feel in control of my world. It was spinning at a dizzying rate, and it left me unsteady and fearful.

32

Something Unexpected

With my divorce underway, I settled on the fact that I would probably be single for the rest of my life, investing my time and the whole of my being in keeping the support network afloat and teaching parenting classes. The school session was rounding up, and contentment washed over me. But still, a tiny twinge of desire to be in a loving and committed relationship remained. It worsened when I could see it all around me but was getting none specifically for myself. Daily worrying about it wasn't proffering any solution, so I prayed from the depths of my soul while driving one day.

"Lord," I cried out, my need evident in my voice. "You know, if you want me to stay single and be a support to these women, I'm willing to do that. I just need you to let me know somehow. But if you have someone for me, I need a sign to confirm if he is from you. So, let's do it this way. If he is a biker who rides a Harley, loves beer, and loves Jesus, then I will know he is from you." I knew I was rambling, but it wasn't my fault for trying to ensure I wouldn't make a mistake again with such specific requirements. I wanted someone who could also love my children and treat them with the fatherly respect and care they deserved. But regardless of my particular needs, I was sure the Lord would not bring anything less than that into my life.

I continued my work with the women in the program but caring for women and girls was a daily habit I practiced wherever I went, even in my neighborhood. It went beyond the confines of an organization.

A young girl with beautiful red hair lived in my community and became like a daughter to me. She needed a place to stay, unable to reside with her father, who had a die-hard drunk. I had hired her a few times as my babysitter to help out, but with her housing situation growing acute, I offered to have her stay in our home. There was no official arrangement as to her becoming my foster child, but she was clear on her stance to go nowhere near her drunken father. Her being under my roof was kept as an informal agreement.

Her father and I became friends along the line because we had to constantly communicate about Elise. We also had to meet frequently in order for me to collect the financial support he provided for her care. Elise was sweet and beautiful, but she was also a handful. She was 15 when she came to live with me, and her discovery of the opposite sex was a novel idea to her, captivating and intriguing. We talked a lot about the boys she was interested in and the ones she thought were interested in her, because I thought it was the best way to keep her open with me. But then Elise started sneaking out without telling me where she was going. Very conversant with all that was bound to follow, I was determined not to allow her to get pregnant on my watch.

I spent a lot of time talking to her father about how to care for Elise. It finally came out that, although he was a prejudiced white man and I, a black woman, he liked me romantically. I explained that I wanted nothing more than friendship but would be willing to hang out together as long as he was sober. He accepted my condition, taking me to many biker events because I had always been fascinated with motorcycles and the people who rode them. While we were out together, we talked about Elise and how she was always sneaking out or skipping school. It was a problem we both shared. Maybe it was one of the reasons our friendship grew.

Back at home, though, I realized I had to sit with Elise and break the news to her that her destructive behavior was too disruptive to the organized life we were used to in my home. "You must go back to your father's house," I told her bluntly.

"No!" she protested, putting up all the walls she had up when we had first met. "I can't go back and live with my dad. I won't! You know why!"

"I know you are upset, darling, but I am too. You are doing things I can't have going on in my home. There are young kids here, and you don't seem to consider that."

I packed up her things and took her home. But even as I walked her to the doorstep, I knew she wasn't going to stay there. On my way home, I felt grief take its course as I asked myself if I had done all I possibly could for her before giving up. I figured that the reason for my grief wasn't that, but rather because I wouldn't be able to make decisions for her to keep her on the right track. But it wasn't mine to make; Elise had to make them for herself. Thankfully, she talked to her older sister in Illinois, and they agreed she should come to her place instead. Elise finished schooling with her older sister and called me regularly to pass messages on to her dad. She refused to do the task herself, preferring to have me send him her regards.

The situation was a strange and unforeseen one. I knew I was attracted to Elise's father, but he was not the man I had prayed for. So, I kept moving forward with an open heart, expecting the signs I had mentioned in my prayers to God. One day, I was cooking on the grill and had treated myself to a couple of glasses of wine when Elise called.

"Hey," she said calmly. "I need my dad. Can you go find him and get him in touch with me?"

"Of course," I was mildly pleased, seeing that she was finally ready to speak to her dad. "Do you need money or something?" I questioned, making sure it was nothing urgent that I could help with. When she replied in the negative, I put my food away and went in search of her father, stopping by all the little biker joints we visited during our outings. But he was nowhere to be found. I stopped at Hawg Stop, the bar that had become our favorite spot.

"Hey!" I called out to the regulars and the bartender. "Have y'all seen One Beer, Mike?" He had earned that nickname from brewing beer in his bathtub. He used to make his own bathtub brew, drinking before heading to the bars for two more cans of beer, passing out right after. They all responded in the negative; no one had seen him. I was weary of running from beer joint to beer joint trying to track down Elise's father and decided to sit there for a few minutes before continuing my search.

I sat and soaked up the atmosphere at the Hawg Stop. It was an excellent place to be, with its authentic biker bar, on a beautiful and fabulously landscaped earth. It featured a large pond, a amphitheater, and great food, with live music three times a week. I happened to be there on one of those nights.

As I sat drinking my beer, I noticed a guy walk in. Our eyes met for the briefest of seconds, and he shook his head, sauntering off in the direction of the pisser. He walked right back out a few minutes later, taking a seat beside me at the bar. I thought he was very attractive, and we struck up a conversation easily, going over my reason for being there at that time. My eyes wandered over his body as he spoke, taking it all in. He had some interesting tattoos that piqued my curiosity. They reminded me of my thoughts of getting a tattoo, but I couldn't decide what kind I wanted to get. It was funny how our conversation turned into a lengthy discussion of tattoos. Minutes turned into hours as we exchanged stories, but it felt like a fleeting moment since our eyes first met.

Terry revealed that he had been married three times, going over the stories surrounding his marriages. As he talked about his ex-wives, he never called them by names, but instead referred to them as numbers one, two, and three. I found that amusing, laughing out loud each time he did it. But at the same time, I was a bit distressed. Did all his failed relationships mean that Terry was unable to make a relationship work?

I started firing questions at him, which he was perfectly willing to answer. His openness and honesty were unexpected and refreshing, and he didn't strike me as a man who sought to hide his past or flaws. He seemed to want me to see and accept him for who he was. If I couldn't, he would know it early in any relationship, before his heart got entangled with mine.

Terry married his first wife when they were seventeen, remaining that way for quite a while. The only issue was that he had cheated on her repeatedly. When they got into their twenties, Terry realized how foolish it was to cheat on his wife and started committing to fidelity. But just when he made that decision, she started having an affair, paying him back in his own coin. Terry confronted her about cheating, but she was ready for his comments.

"I learned from the best," was her only statement, and Terry knew it was all his fault. It was a sobering wake-up call to him about the consequences of his actions. He tried to get the marriage back on track for years, but the damage was already done. It hadn't taken her long before she asked him for a divorce.

He moved on to number two, as he called her, loving profoundly and swearing he would never cheat again. It was surprising that he kept that promise, as I had learned from Matthew that an addict never changes his ways. Maybe Terry was different. Unfortunately, tragedy struck, and he was involved in a terrible motorcycle accident that left him in a coma for months. His second wife was unwilling to wait around to see if he would be in a vegetative state for the rest of his life. He had sustained severe head injuries, and the doctors warned her that people with head injuries often exhibit explosive anger. That was all the conviction she needed to file for divorce.

Along came wife number three, a beautiful-souled individual who led him to church and a relationship with the Lord. She had experienced her transformation story, having found God and gotten herself off drugs. But after they married, she constantly relapsed, exhibiting violence at each peak. She hit him frequently until he couldn't take it anymore. Terry decided then that they could no longer be together, as they had become too toxic. However, they remained good friends since she was the one who led him to Christ.

I asked what brought him to the Hawg Stop that night because I was a regular and had never seen him there before. It was as unexplainable to him as it was to me as he narrated how he felt an urge to come there that evening. It made me ponder carefully about how our worlds collided that evening and how odd it was for me to be there right when he felt pressed to go. Like a high schooler, I started to wonder if it could be true that this was someone I was destined to meet. I set my fairy tale fantasies aside and allowed myself to just enjoy the moment.

Terry offered to give me a ride on his bike sometime. In that culture, that phrase could mean so many things, but I looked into his eyes and judged his intentions to be honorable. And one glance out the window at his bike, I sure did want to ride it with him. Maybe that was why I handed him my card and invited him to call me sometime, keeping my fingers crossed. We left it there and said goodbye.

As I got comfortable in my car, adjusting the seatbelt straps so I could go home, my heart flew above me a thousand feet in the sky. I felt compelled to return and have one more can of non-alcoholic beer with him. I found him sitting at the bar, staring at my business card. He was wearing the most awkward look on his face, and I was glad he had not already shoved it into his wallet. It meant he was interested.

"Hey," I said, interrupting his pensive thoughts. "I want you to call me, okay? Make sure you do."

He looked up at me, saying nothing for a few seconds. "Let me walk you out," he finally uttered, standing, taking my arm, and wrapping it around his.

I was thrilled to be walking alongside him in his black leather chaps that did little to hide his muscular frame. I gently felt the well-defined muscle of where our conversation on tattoos began, but my staring had to end all too soon. On reaching my car, he looked at me with the same awkward look he had on his face at the bar.

"Tyra, can I steal a kiss?" He asked playfully, playing with my hair under the night sky. I didn't seem to mind because it felt like something he should have been doing. It felt so natural.

"You can," I responded with a soft whisper.

We shared a brief kiss that sent my heart fluttering, and instantly, I knew I had found my beer-drinking, Harley-riding, Jesus-loving man! Strangely enough, he shares the story of our meeting entirely differently to this day. It was as if we were in an alternate universe. We each remember different versions of the story, as if God was tailor-making each of our experiences to be exactly what we both needed.

The few preceding days were calm and lazy, a welcomed respite from my ordinarily busy life. I decided to log into my Facebook account and immediately received a friend request from him. Our daily conversations started, and I found myself wanting to hear from him more than the average human in my life. I saw that he would post check-ins regularly, many of which were pictures of him at church. It was exciting to scroll through those images taken from various angles, marveling at my luck.

Then the day came when I got the message I had been waiting for: *"Hey, let me know whenever you want to go on that ride."*

Our weeks were hectic, but we both had the weekend off, so a date was fixed. But our first few days together did not involve zipping down the highway on his *hawg*, with the screaming wind caressing my hair. Instead, we returned to the Hawg Stop, where it all began, sharing stories and cans of beer. During one of those dates, he had a severe look. And reflexively, I braced myself for what he would say next.

"I have to be honest with you before we take this any further," Terry pensively said, staring me in the eyes.

My heart pounded in my chest, and my thoughts went haywire. *Where is he about to go with this? He better not have a girlfriend or a wife or something like that.*

"I want to ensure that you know and understand that I am a born-again and only came to the Hawg Stop because I felt compelled to come that night," I could see traces of where he was headed. "Mostly, I ride alone and go to different biking spots. I want to make sure that you know I am a Christian. Whoever I also date has to be a Christian and a non-smoker." He took a deep breath, as if he was relieved to finally get that out.

I lit up, grinning so hard I thought my teeth were going to break. Terry was everything I hoped and prayed for. He didn't know that I had been checking his Facebook and saw that he went to church twice weekly. If he knew, he would probably have discovered that he was the perfect image of what I had been praying for.

Thursday was our date night, and I looked forward to being with Terry, going on our little excursions out of town. Before long, the holidays came around. There is a little more excitement when there is a new love at Christmas time. It brought the holidays to life in a beautiful way.

Terry was a big holiday guy and loved the festivities surrounding Christmas. He invited me over to his home for a holiday bonfire, and I drove from Houston to Conroe, excited to enjoy my time with him. As I journeyed that day, the scenery became more rural with every turn I made. The properties were spread out over the countryside, with farms stretched as far as the eye could see. But there were very few houses. As I neared his property, there was little to identify if it was supposed to be the location of a home. Then the GPS signaled it was time for me to turn.

Turn? Into what?

Moving down the driveway, my eyes scanned the landscape. I could only see a little trailer sitting on a couple of acres of land surrounded by boats and motorcycles.

Should I turn around and get out of there?

I had no idea what to expect but kept going when I caught sight of him in the area behind the trailer getting the bonfire ready. He had seen me already, so turning back wasn't an option. The beauty of the land greeted me as my feet touched down. It was positioned alongside a creek, and the sound of the babbling water immediately relaxed my nerves. I was so stunned by its beauty that all my initial reservations were forgotten. Terry and I had a lovely bonfire and spent several hours talking and getting to know one another more intimately.

As the night wore on, I wondered what his intentions for the remainder of the evening were. I knew that he was a Christian, but I also knew plenty of Christian men who were not opposed to having an intimate relationship before marriage. He had done me the favor of being honest about what he was looking for that night in the bar, early in our relationship. So, I decided to repay the favor with some straight talk. I wasn't one to stall conversations like this.

"This has been wonderful," I said, breathing in the cool air. "But I think there is something you should know," I recognized the look on Terry's face as the same one I had when he had started a similar conversation with me weeks ago. I smiled reassuringly and continued. "I am not having sex with anyone, so I hope that is not what you are looking for."

He smiled and shook his head. "You're still married," he accurately pointed out. "So, I wouldn't touch you anyway."

I was satisfied with that response and thrilled at his integrity. We dated for a couple of months after that, content with hanging out on weekends and going on rides together. Then, one evening, he asked me a cryptic question.

"I am thinking about building a house on my property," he said, referring to the expanse of land where we'd had the bonfire. "A Tiny

House isn't such a bad idea, right? Or, do think I should just get a full sized house?"

"That's great," I replied. It would alienate the fear of driving down the lonely path each time. "Those are so nice. I've heard a lot about them."

Terry laughed, then suddenly became very serious. "So, what do you think of my plan?"

"What do I think?" I questioned, thinking about the meaning of the question. Then it hit me. Terry was not necessarily asking what I thought about his plan. He was asking about our future and whether or not I could see myself living in a pretty small house or whether he should consider increasing the size of the house to accommodate my family and me. The question was a gauge of our future together.

After that question, I quickly contacted my attorney and ensured he rushed through the divorce proceedings. With my divorce finalized, Terry asked me to marry him the following weekend. Two months after that, I was married to my beer-drinking, Harley-riding, Jesus-loving man.

33

Nothing is without Challenges

As every typical newlywed, my life revolved around making our new family work. It was almost like the usual, but this time without a husband who smoked pot at every opportunity. But on the other hand, my oldest son, Cameron, came home stoned after being reported smoking marijuana in school. The school he attended was in a depressed neighborhood, and drugs were prevalent. Thus, there were little walls set up between his teenage excessiveness and its means. His mood was changing, with his demeanor growing more and more combative. He had always been an incredible, calm, collected kid who loved church, school, and family. But as his drug habit worsened, being that kid became more difficult.

At the same time, my second oldest, Nicole, was acting out. An arduous kid to manage, her behavior was unpredictable and somewhat troubling. She was transforming rapidly from a sweetheart to something more on the opposite side, intent on rebelling against me and every other authority figure. It was so bad that she had no problem calling me a bitch to my face. Worse, she started taking an interest in boys, which brought about a whole new set of issues, given my experience with that. It was a mess.

Like any parent, I searched for the root cause of the problem, thinking that if I eradicated the source of all their sudden teenage outburst, I could hit the reset button and have my perfect, angelic children back again. But life doesn't work that way; children are not meant to be perfect. You sometimes discover an issue with your children long after the damage is done. You can only start from the point you are accustomed to, repairing the breach until the cracks become invincible.

So, constantly drug testing my son became our first step in patching up the spotted cracks, but we were far from getting either one of them back on track. We laid the blame at the feet of the neighborhood we were living in, as the joints lining up the street corners and the provocative stares of the ladies at dark spots weren't something that was particularly hidden. We thought things would improve if we could get the children into a better community and school, but the house on the property Terry owned was too far away from completion. So, I suggested we temporarily move to the travel trailer while the house was under construction. I had adapted to living there already, so we purchased a second one where two of the four kids stayed, and Terry, Annalisa, and Andrew lived in the other. We thought it would be a temporary solution, lasting only three months. But eighteen months later, we were all still cramped in the same travel trailers, and things had grown worse than before. Nicole was angry about the move, blaming Terry for the changes that were happening in her life. Her daddy issues were glaring for us all to see, but Terry didn't deserve that treatment.

As if that wasn't enough, my ex-husband resurfaced, arranging for a visitation schedule for his two youngest children. He refused the first two being a part of his visits, disregarding that he had been instrumental in raising them for more than half of their lives. This rejection further tore Nicole's feelings apart. Her father was a professional soccer player who was always on the road. As a result, they had a troubled relationship that her father couldn't manage alongside his busy schedule. Nicole was strong-willed and blunt, and her father refused to tolerate it, unlike Terry, who was patient and kind for the longest time.

One day, Nicole got in trouble, and I punished her by taking her phone. That made her furious, responding by screaming obscenities at me. Terry, watching the whole exchange happen, was not happy with that. Naturally, he decided to talk to her about it, but it only ended up being a bumping of heads in a big way. During another incident, Nicole wanted something that I was bent on not handing over to her, so she started yelling and swearing loud enough that Terry heard her from outside. He came in angry, demanding that she return to her travel trailer. Nicole refused, and Terry decided to do the task himself.

My daughter fought back, refusing to be dominated and controlled that way. Terry fell back, trying to get her into the trailer, and Nicole fell on top of him. The commotion was so loud that the other children came running to see what was happening. In the end, we were able to get her out of our trailer, but knowing Nicole, she was far from done. She stood outside the trailer, cussing and fussing at both of us like we were the sole reason she was always angry and spiteful. I came out to calm her down, contradicting Terry's warnings, and remind her that she couldn't talk to her parents that way. Nicole couldn't care less as she lunged toward me, continuing to rant and rave. I slapped her, and she slapped back, like two high schoolers fighting over a man. The second brawl was on, sending Nicole and me to the ground, rolling around in the dirt.

She got up off the ground as if nothing had happened, looking me in the eye. The words that preceded stunned the entire family.

"I'm pregnant!" she suddenly screamed.

"Oh hell!" I whispered to myself. I didn't see how this wasn't going to hurt Nicole, as well as the rest of my family. Her mood changes and erratic behavior all began to make more sense to me. I ran to the phone and called her boyfriend's home, needing to speak to his mother, Wendy, about what Nicole had just spilled to the entire family.

"Nicole says she's pregnant," I still couldn't believe I was saying those words. "You need to come to get her!"

But Nicole was not pregnant. After a visit to the doctor, I discovered that she was still a virgin. Apparently, my daughter's sudden rash behavior was because she was angry at not being allowed to be with her boyfriend whenever she wanted to. We also learned that her boyfriend had been trying to convince her to come live with him, so her actions were the grounds she needed to get out of my house. And it worked like magic. They came for her, as we didn't have the space for that kind of crazy. Nicole did ultimately get pregnant several months later.

But our challenges weren't over in the slightest, as they seemed to arise at every turn we reached. This time around, it was a job situation. Our move meant that I was 50 miles away from the school I loved but closer to one that could hardly afford to pay me what I was worth. Not having any other choice, I accepted a $6,000 pay cut that caused our family budget to wobble, considering the fact that we had a house under construction. There was also my trying to adapt to the system of the new school. As a behavior specialist, one might think the teachers would appreciate the help they were getting, but they always seemed to raise an eyebrow when they met me and were further shocked to learn that I had entered the field voluntarily. They were floored when I confessed that I loved it!

We made a lot of sacrifices to get Cameron away from the drug issues he faced, our move being one of them, but he found other means of getting his daily dosage in our new area. Though he was doing much better, it was still stressful for us all. He successfully made it to his senior year in high school, but I felt the need to check on his wellbeing at intervals. There was always a chance of a relapse.

There was so much I had to take charge of, but it was always to the detriment of another. Something had to give. I called Claiborne School District to talk to them about a job. I was taken aback when the Human Resources Director informed me that she was also the head of the special education department. The school district was so small that she had to run both offices simultaneously. Getting a copy of my resume, she sent out word to the schools in the district, and in a few seconds, my phone was ringing off the hook with offers. I was interviewed and hired on the spot. But I wasn't even allowed to be excited as the principal abruptly stepped in with caution.

"There is one student I should mention to you because she may end up with you. Her name is Renee," the principal called her name with such fervor, as if she was someone to be feared. "She is not here and probably won't be right away. But trust me, she will be coming."

I was puzzled at the principal's weird welcoming remark. I knew behavior like the back of my hand and was quite an expert at transforming behaviors into positive channels. It was boldly written in my resume, so it definitely meant more than that if she had thought to mention it. So, I pondered long and hard about this warning.

What are they trying to tell me? A student with behavior problems? Hello? That is what I do.

I should have taken the hint that this was no ordinary behavioral concern. I would soon learn that this student was legendary, but for all the wrong reasons.

34

The Voice

I accepted the new job, not bothering to consider the pay rate. It was more than enough being so close to home that nothing else mattered. I was so focused on avoiding working far from home that I forgot to even ask about the salary, and of course, the things we neglect are the ones we end up regretting. After I resigned from my previous position and accepted my new contract, I saw that I would earn less than I did in my last job. That development ad lack of scrutiny on my part further strained our already tight budget, adding tension to my marriage and our family. Coupled with that was the stress of the travel trailers and their maintenance. It couldn't have taken a more arduous toil on me.

In my first week at my new job, I noticed people talking in hushed voices whenever I was around. Although I noticed it despite their attempts to hide it, I decided not to give it any more thought, as it didn't really come up on my list priorities.

I made new friends with 2 other staff members in the school, a newly employed worker and assistant of mine, Miss Green, and the amiable school nurse. Our friendship grew so fast in a short time, getting to a point where we were certain that we could rely on one another, without becoming burdensome. In the little space between us, Miss Green kept telling me of a rumor she heard about something called "the voice." The nurse and I tried to figure out what this meant by asking around, but no one seemed to want to give an ample explanation. It was getting on my nerves and it only worsened when someone approached me to ask if I had heard of "the voice." Even after voicing out my confusion in a frustrated tone, the only response I got was a cryptic, "you'll see." What was I supposed to be seeing?

In my first year, I meticulously kept written documentation on student behavior. With a couple of boys in the program doing well, the notes seemed to be paying off. But one day, Renee, the student I had been warned about, came in. I instantly recalled what the principal had said, and I wondered, for the umpteenth time, how bad it could possibly get. Usually, students came in with common behavioral issues that sprang from emotional trauma, but I discovered that this fourth grader was different. Her problems were off the chart.

For starters, she didn't speak much, content on remaining in her own space, observing in a weird fashion. She was highly withdrawn, her dark and fearful eyes moving around as if she had been cast in a horror movie. Renee wore heavy makeup to intensify her appearance, making her look frightened but, at the same time, frightening. But the worst part was her extreme violence. I could not figure out why the school had placed a child with such heavy issues in my class, especially since she was not well matched with her peers or any of the teaching staff. Kids with minor life skills are intellectually deficient, some of them mentally or developmentally challenged, with autism or down syndrome. But in the behavior program, there were kids who were intellectually at an average level but with high anger issues. To have a child in my classroom whose concerns were at this level of severity was odd. In my quest to figure out what I was missing, I learned that her violence caused her to be placed with me and away from the students in the life skills area.

Renee was a full-time job, I admit. At odd times, she would get up and run toward the door to leave the room, and each time, she got us running, too, trying to bring her back. It always ended with her striking out, hitting either my assistant or me. There was one time when she went to the bathroom, spending more time than was necessary there. I noticed because I had to pay utmost attention to her, so I went to the doors, trying to persuade her to come out. My feet halted when I heard a strangely deep voice behind the door, shouting curses to God. She was talking nonstop, her language dotted with profanity. It was *the voice*. Renee's face completely changed when she emerged from the bathroom, curses still pouring from her lips. She looked like a different person, and not in a good way. It was terrifying.

My assistant and I were furious that we had been put in this position, knowing it was intentionally assigned to my classroom. On a brighter note, we knew what we were dealing with when we heard the voice. But there was a minus. I had dealt with violent children before, but this was different. I knew I had no other means but my daily regimen: to pray for my classroom, the students, and the staff before the start of each day. Through prayer, my training, hard work, and perseverance, I was always successful in helping my students acclimate.

But for Renee, I prayed over time, yet, there was no change. If anything, she was getting worse with the passing of every day. She evolved to tying her arms and legs to the chairs or tables, seemingly obsessed with being tied up like an animal. It was only a natural train of thought that we wondered if her father had been tying her up after all the wild stories, we had heard of her from the class, including when she had gone missing for some time and was found living under a neighbor's trailer.

Multiple CPS cases were opened, and it was discovered that her father had restraints to keep her under control. Maybe I needed that with her, too, because I was beginning to feel like I needed help. A good day meant I was struck and bruised, while the bad days required a visit to the doctor or a hospital. Renee tore my rotator cuff and a bicep and caused me to have bone spurs. Intensive mental health care was sought for her, and she was taken to the hospital multiple times. Once, they kept her for a couple of weeks, providing the students and staff with a much-needed respite. But it was not their practice to keep children there when not on a strict medical watch. In the end, they let her go, and then she was back in the classroom, ending the reprieve for the students and staff.

That year was the most hectic year in my profession. My faith and skills were tested, my perfect track record blemished, but my heart ached for Renee. I prayed earnestly at sunrise, hurt seeing her that way.

What is wrong with my salvation that my prayers are not answered, Renee? Please help me help her, Lord.

Teachers believed she was a living case of demon possession, and they could not be faulted for that belief. Whatever it was, I no longer felt I could handle it, so I contacted Pasadena School District, and the officials there were happy to take me back. There was only one problem - Claiborne refused to release me from my contract. They maintained that they had to get an applicant for my position before I could be let out of contract, and as a minor step toward appeasing me, they placed Renee and me in an empty room. There were no chairs to throw or tables for her to tie herself to. Only windows and shelves acted as decors in the room. Why hadn't they thought of this sooner?

One day, Renee turned pale and started to throw up. We immediately rushed a trash can over to her, but she turned away from it, content to do it all over the classroom. When we tried to get her to throw up in the trash can instead, she let out a sinister and wicked laugh in that dark, deep voice we had heard and grown accustomed to. The vomit suddenly turned projectile, aiming for us. Miss Green ran to the door, her instincts telling her to run to safety. I called her to come back and help me, but Miss Green remained by the door, desperately shaking her head. She was just too frightened to be reasoned with. I returned my attention to Renee as she continued to laugh, begging her to aim at the can instead of me. It was a day that never left my memory.

One afternoon, I was listening to a radio show. The scripture the guest read was Mark 9:25-29: When Jesus saw that the people came running together, He rebuked the unclean spirit, saying to it, "Deaf and dumb spirit, I command you, come out of him and enter him no more!" Then the spirit cried out, convulsed him greatly, and came out of him. And he became as one dead, so that many said, "He is dead." But Jesus took him by the hand, lifted him, and arose. And when He had come into the house,

His disciples asked Him privately, "Why could we not cast it out?" So, He said to them, "This kind can come out by nothing but prayer and fasting."

I was shaken to my core by listening to the radio that day. I took that scripture and made it my mantra, using it as often as I could. I made twenty-five copies of the scriptures while Renee was in the hospital and taped them throughout my classroom. I placed them under every chair and desk, in cabinets, and in every other place where I was certain no one could easily see them.

Renee returned to school after one of her many episodes. We weren't sure she if was even going to return with the level of possession she portrayed in her last episode, but there she was. I knew it was destined to be a bad morning the moment she stepped into the classroom with "the look." We kept a strict routine at the school because these kids needed structure, but that morning, we could not get Renee started on her process, which included eating her breakfast, handwriting, computer work, and group lessons. She would not even take a seat.

I sat at my desk working with the other two students who had improved so much that they would have a couple of mainstream classes that day. Renee stalked the classroom, walking around the space and glaring menacingly at us. We expected that, at any moment, the fireworks would begin, so I got the other two students off to their classes and invited Renee to sit with me. We kept watching her from a little distance, giving her the space, I knew she wanted.

Then the eeriest thing happened.

Renee stopped, froze for a few seconds, bent over, and pulled one of the scriptures from under the chair. She had not been there when they were placed and had never looked under the chairs before. But somehow, Renee knew it was there. She held the paper in her hand for a moment before walking over and handing it to me. I had forgotten that I had placed the scripture around the room a couple of weeks prior and was shocked and a bit terrified about what would happen next. But unexpectedly, Renee calmly walked over to her seat and started working. Miss Green and I looked at one another, completely speechless.

At that moment, my faith soared sky high. It had nothing to do with my lack of spirituality, as I was doing the right thing, but I did not understand that I was waging war against spiritual forces. God was listening to me, working on Renee's behalf. I rushed to tell my supervisor what had happened, and she confessed that it was a chilling story and that it had significantly impacted her. We established a staff prayer meeting and invited anyone who wanted to come. We ended up having two sessions to accommodate everyone. Word spread throughout the building about this incident with Renee, and almost everyone wanted to be involved with it.

Renee was the girl no one wanted to interact with, but after that, she sat and worked like a regular student. I wanted to talk to her parents, but their status as not being religious was a deterring factor for me. So, we were content in rejoicing over her successes, as she now aced spelling tests, finished her work, and talked more often. Although there was the occasional outburst where she took a swing at me, they grew fewer and farther apart. Renee had changed.

We finished the year in some semblance of peace, but my rotator cuff injury was worsening, with the pain growing so intense that I would lose consciousness for a while. I saw an orthopedic doctor who advised that only surgery could fix it. I was in a fixer.

I had been entrenched in the classroom for so long in such difficult circumstances that the weekends were like being released from a dangerous prison. On Sunday nights, the thought of returning to school permeated my mind, sending me into a panic attack. Ironically, although I was declining fast, I performed stellar each time I was at work. It took therapy for me to uncover that I was angry about what the school had done in allowing this child to be underserved in the way she was. I had been certified to teach, but when students have a label, they get protected while the teachers remain exposed. And I had become a victim of that lack of protection.

35

Doc. Hodge

I continued to practice behavioral interventions, but my dream of being a behavioral specialist had not yet been realized. Finding it along the path to wherever God was leading was all I hoped on. There was nothing for a long while, until an opening at a nearby school district suddenly offered some promise. With the hope I had grown so accustomed to in hand, I went for the interviewed and was hired. One of my many career goals had finally been actualized.

But there was still one I was yet to accomplish, and it sat there, demanding some attention. Nearly three years had passed since I had done any more work toward my doctorate. I was so caught up in Terry, my family, and my job that there had been no time to do anything else, aside from publishing several excellent books, including a teacher devotional and a dating book. I also continued to speak occasionally. Still, the anxiety of the past haunted me. I was still sure Mary would suddenly appear in my life like a mugger leaping from the shadows. I identified it as an irrational fear, but most fears are. Mine exacerbated my anxiety.

But my fear aside, this new job brought a different type of joy; the money was great, and my boss was excellent. But I had some conflicts with the school psychologist, who constantly contradicted and countermanded me. I was the head of the behavioral programs, and my job specification included hosting pieces of training. One such day, she stood in the middle of my training and took over the class, completely marginalizing me. We were all shocked, and my staff kept staring at the both of us, trying to figure out what was happening. The moment I let it slip that I was angry, the teacher I talked to rushed back to the administration to report me for allowing my feelings about this teacher to be known, and I was disciplined.

I put the incident behind me, deciding to focus on my doctorate, now that it seemed I had the time. I submitted my papers in preparation for my pre-defense, but they just kept getting kicked back to me to clean up areas the committee had issues with. There wasn't ample time to make the corrections, especially when two new students with problems similar to Renee's were introduced to my workload. One of the boys believed that the devil instructed him to kill, drag, and hang black women. At the time, I was the only black woman in the district, so it is understandable why I had certain reservations.

When I visited, the boy was acting strangely. He took his backpack and put it in the rear corner, away from where all the other students had placed their backpacks. I had a teacher call him out of the room, suspicious that he was hiding something in it. On searching his backpack, I came up with a butcher knife, and I was not exactly shocked, given his behavioral pattern. Several administrators and I conducted an interview with him, where he confessed his intention to kill.

My hands were full; it was no wonder that my pre-defense was rejected. I had rushed through it, trying to meet the deadline and, at the same time, overwhelmed from work. But I was determined to see it through despite all odds. I was supposed to meet with the committee online on the day of my defense. However, it seemed that everything that could possibly go wrong, did in fact, go wrong. I had a problem with getting connected online and had to find an internet connection elsewhere, which caused me to be late for my dissertation defense. I was beyond embarrassed, but the committee was gracious enough to wait for me and my defense.

One of the professors spoke up at the end of the meeting after my hurriedly prepared and delivered speech. "I don't feel comfortable giving you a doctorate," she said, her voice echoing through my phone. "I just don't think you are ready. I don't see you getting it. I don't see myself ever giving you a doctorate"

I broke down completely, having spent so much time and money trying to get something that looked terrifyingly far from my reach. I went to bed that night with a roll of tissue beside my bed and got out the next morning with puffy eyes. The following day, I went to work early to pray, as I had been doing for years. Opening my computer, I saw that some new Google documents had been shared with me over Google docs by the same psychologist who opposed me and hijacked my training. It was a new medium at the time, and people were still learning how to use it. That would have been the only reason why she had done that without realizing that I had access to the paper through our shared permission and would be able to see everything she had sent.

I watched in real time as she edited the information in the document, not understanding why the numbers were being changed. The next day, I was called into a meeting with the supervisor to address a complaint from the psychologist that I had failed to inform her about a student suffering from regression. The information on the Google doc had been presented as evidence of the student's decline, but since I had watched her change the numbers, I knew the information was falsified. Staring blankly at my supervisor, I demanded the source files to prove that a fraud had been committed. My boss yelled at me.

"Why would anyone do that?" she screamed with her hands flailing. "Why would you make such an accusation?"

"You're right," I answered calmly. "Why would anyone do that?" At that moment, my decision had already been made. Taking my leave, I went home and wrote my resignation letter to be effective at the end of the school year. I wanted to give them enough time to find the best person to replace me.

I returned to my former district, learning that significant growth was heading its way. It was reported that a considerable change was happening, and I could tell they would need someone like me. But the question of my dissertation loomed largely. Would I be able to do both: working and defending my dissertation? The only way to find out was to delve into it, as no answers were awaiting me on the sidelines.

The position I accepted at the new school was in a DAEP - Disciplinary Alternative Behavioral Program, and I was totally in love with the place. The program was designed especially for suspended or expelled students, and only students with an assault or drug offense qualified for it. I had a great supervisor, my workload was heavy but manageable, and my students were terrific, giving me the chance to help them as much as I possibly could. I had a well-structured classroom, with a variety of students ranging from gang members and teen parents to drug addicts, who didn't behave for anyone else except for me. I helped kids catch up through credit recovery. They asked me to play music, and I responded with spiritual songs to help encourage them.

I was named the "Super Lady of the Year" for the city of Houston.

Finally, my mind was back on the dissertation. I started over and formed a new committee, retaining only the chair because he had the best reputation for getting students through the process. I spent the better part of a year finishing my rewrite, working all day, and returning home at night to write. It was a struggle for the whole family because, while I was studying, they had to get by entirely without me.

My kids came up with clever ways to get my attention during those years that I was studying for my master's degree and my doctorate. When my daughter was about four or five years old, she taught herself how to do some amazing backflips. It looked like she would land on her head, but, at the last minute, she'd get her legs under her and complete the flip perfectly. Still, it would make me so nervous that my eyes would never leave her until I was sure she was safe. When I was working on my degrees, she and her sister would be in the same room, and she would do one of these flips while I was studying from a corner.

They made me so scared that she would get hurt that I finally told her to stop. "I don't want you doing flip-flops until I can get you trained." I voiced my reservations, and she listened to me. A while later, she got professionally trained and became a cheerleader for her school.

My other daughter would play loud music and start doing wild dance moves, and I could swear she was doing it to get me to look over at her. When I finally looked up, she would do a hand jive to make her fingers look strange, pretending she wasn't making a whole lot of moves just moments prior. As soon as I looked away, she would start dancing again. It was hilarious watching her in my peripheral vision.

In November, I was finally ready to defend before the committee again. The committee members threw tough questions at me, but I was able to answer them all. After that stage, I had to wait patiently without disintegrating from anticipation as the committee silenced the zoom and turned off their cameras to discuss whether or not I was successful.

When they returned to the zoom, Dr. Sims spoke first. "OK, Dr. Hodge…"

I felt like I was floating on air. I had done it! Hearing the title "Doctor" as an affix to my name was powerful, and I immediately went live on Facebook to share the news with everyone. In December 2018, I graduated.

I had promised my supervisor that I would stay two years at the school no matter what happened, and the fact that I had my doctorate could not change things. I continued to work diligently, getting rewarded with an excellent contract commensurate with my skills and experience, along with some stipends and other perks. God's favor was all over the place.

In the second year I had committed to the school, the district had a change in superintendents. In a meeting with him, I inadvertently called him out about the perks being offered to new people when there were individuals who loved the district and had served faithfully for years. My sudden outburst caused him to wonder about the identity of the outspoken lady, thinking I was being confrontational. But I wasn't. I simply wanted the district to think more carefully about what was right and fair.

He approached me one day. "So, tell me what you do here?"

"I do whatever is needed," I responded, cheeky as always. "I am my supervisor's right arm and I do whatever needs doing."

"So, you are his go-to person?" He questioned again.

"Right!" I nodded. "On some days, I complete reports. On other days, I accompany students to the alternative school and help teachers with behavioral issues in the classroom."

I was so busy working hard that conversations were being had in my absence about my career and a promotion that I knew nothing about at the time. I had several students who had no chance of graduating on time that were placed in DAEP, so we had to work like maniacs to get them caught up so they could graduate. I pushed them, stayed late, and worked with them one-on-one, and in the end, they all did a fantastic job, with graduation in sight. A part of my plan was to insist that each student maintain a journal, as it helped to keep them focused.

There was a bright student, in particular, that got my attention. He was a gangbanger, but he always got his work done. I couldn't figure out what it was, but I felt something was wrong with him. Another student, Joey, was clearly troubled and constantly involved in crimes around the city. Whenever there was an incident in town, there was a high probability that he was knee-deep into it. One morning, I came in to find that neither student was present, later finding out that Zack had shot and killed Joey.

I was devastated.

My boss called me in, handing over Joey's journal. It detailed his life story in such a poignant manner, sharing how much of a struggle it was to work, try to stay on a straight path, and get up each day to go to school. He shared how his mother was struggling daily to make a living and how he worked a legitimate job at What-A-Burger. But when the money got tight, he would go out into the streets to get what was needed to help take care of his family. He wrote about how much he wanted to make it and do good for his mother.

Sometime earlier, I learned that I have the gift of discernment, one of the gifts of the Holy Spirit. I would get a sense of who kids were and what they were all about, no matter how nondescript and regular they looked. I took a deep dive into the bible, learning how to use my gifts, improving my prayer life, and calling out each student's name to God daily.

Another student, Andrew, had come to Texas from California with a boxcutter in his waistband. He was in bad educational shape, starting with just three credits toward graduation and needing a total of 26 credits. I would sit him next to my desk each day because I didn't want him to get into conflicts with any of the other students. Sitting near me, he was laser-focused, completing his work and turning three credits into the twenty-three he needed. For years, the teachers and I would joke that students who came in with no shot of graduation would need to be on the Andrew Plan. His journey taught us that anyone could make it to the finish line if they were willing to do the work.

Andrew, however, was always frowning, never seeing a reason to laugh unnecessarily. He was always so serious, too serious even for chasing a chance at graduation. I asked him why he had so much pent-up anger in him.

"I'm mad at God," he answered defiantly. There seemed to have been a lot of hurts behind those words.

"Why?" I wanted a peek into his life. It told more than his outward behavior did.

"My family got involved with the church in California. We were doing well, and I was even thinking of leaving the gang. But then, my cousin had to start sleeping with the pastor's wife. To cover it up, she blackballed my whole family. And just like that, we became outcasts. It was the last time I wanted to have anything to do with the church." His hands clutched into fists as he narrated his experience, and I reached out to ease them.

My heart was broken. All my years as an educator, I never preached at my students or tried to proselytize them. Instead, I let my light and love for them serve as my sermon. So that was what I did with Andrew, too, despite the urge to tell him that God loved him so much.

Andrew was with me the following school year, and his behavior was modifying. He was getting close to being admitted to a school where he could finish his work and graduate.

One day, he suddenly blurted out, "Miss, do you think I should accept God?"

"It's your choice, Andrew," I replied, happy that he had been considering it. "Only you can decide that."

"Do you think I should accept the devil," he tried again.

"No," I said quickly, turning to face him sharply. "Go with God. God is the better choice! If you ever need prayer about anything, I will pray with you. God has a good plan for you. If you choose God's plan, you will always have His strength to help you." It was the most I could tell him, but I hoped it was sufficient.

On one particular day, the new school superintendent was visiting campus when he asked me what I did on campus. "Whatever my boss tells me to do," was my response, but I did not mean it to come out as it did. But it was true that I did everything he told me to do. There were different tasks each day, like helping with a new batch of students, coaching teachers, implementing behavioral strategies, or even being campus supervisor for the day. Whatever he told me to do, I did it.

I later learned that my superintendent had gone to my boss to confirm that everything I said about my work in the district was true, and then some. He asked the same question to my boss and got the same reply.

The superintendent watched me for three months as I worked with the students. During that period, one of the assistants told my supervisor I was being moved to a new position in the district, but I didn't know what that meant. Shortly after COVID broke out, everything was halted for a while, but eventually, I was promoted to the position of high school assistant principal. God was so faithful.

Andrew was admitted to the alternative campus, on track to round up his studies. I had not seen him for months until I was asked to work at a soccer game. I was so surprised and pleased to see him there.

"Hey!" he called out to me, waving his hands excitedly in the air. "I have looked at every game, hoping to find you."

"Hey, Andrew," I grinned so wide that my jaw hurt. "I heard you are on track to becoming a graduate."

"If it weren't for you, I wouldn't be." Andrew was a grateful kid, and that habit was going to take him places.

We hugged and took a picture together. As he walked away, my heart filled with pride. Suddenly, he turned back.

"Hey, Miss?"

"Yes, Andrew?"

"God bless you."

I nearly burst into tears from those few words. Andrew was the fruit of my labor. He graduated later that year, defying all the odds and bringing to life the Andrew Plan. I'll never forget what his life story taught me, as it inspired me as much as I inspired him.

Another student, Yesina, was placed in DAEP for drug use. She was a freshman, already going in the wrong direction in her education and her life in general. Two other girls there hated her for some reason and constantly started conflicts with her. Those girls, with a sick sense of humor, hacked into Yessna's school email and sent out a message threatening to harm everyone at the school. The police intervened and arrested her amidst her protests that she wasn't guilty. I believed her, even though the police and practically everyone else claimed that all guilty people proclaimed innocence. I insisted on an investigation, which led to the discovery of her innocence through the footage of the cameras showing her rivals logging into her computer. Yessna was released from jail.

When she returned, she ran straight to my office. "Miss, thank you for believing in me and fighting for me. My mom was going to put me out over this. You were the only one who believed in me." I wanted to tell her it wasn't just me but the Holy Spirit at work. I could have easily joined the crowned in casting stones at her.

Yessna started catching up on her classes and recovered her credits. After the investigation, she got to see the other two girls taken out of class and arrested for hacking into her email. One of the girls was expelled from DAEP, which meant that there was no other place for her, as DAEP was the last stop on the education train. She was so angry that she started sending threatening messages to the school, threatening to kill everyone.

On the other hand, the last time I spoke to Yessna, she had already caught up with her classes and played volleyball at the high school. She was faring well, another fruit ripe for harvest.

36

Conclusion – Facing Demons

My fulfillment and satisfaction were derived from my job, as the most challenging students no one else could handle were placed on my doorstep because I was uniquely gifted to care for them and try to coax their best selves forward. I often thought about Renee and wondered what had happened to her, whether she was demon-possessed or not. It was indisputable that she had emotional demons plaguing her and was, at times, withdrawn and fearful. Sometimes, Renee would rock and moan in isolation, wanting nothing to do with anyone, while at other times, she was angry, combative, and violent. I saw deep into her soul; her spirit was broken.

    Where Renee was concerned, I was no different from any of the other members of staff. Renee terrified me with the eerie air that enveloped all when she was around. Each day she came in, I would silently pray for her and speak words of life to her dying spirit. I prayed for her mental healing and the courage to help her. Where everyone else gave up, I pressed in.

Renee was ultimately taken away from her dad under the allegations of abuse and neglect. Right now, she is deeply ensconced in the Child Protective Services system. She was moved to a more restricted environment, and I never got to see her again. While others cheered at her departure, I knew they all learned a thing from her and were sad to see her go. I, for one, learned so much from working with her and the others.

I was encouraged to help as many children as possible, realizing I would be more effective as a principal than a teacher. Rather than assist a dozen, I could impact the lives of hundreds in that position. The transition from being a behavior specialist was partly a result of my colleagues who pushed me to consider it. Usually, I didn't see myself as a principal; I didn't think I was good enough. Like Renee, I had demons that haunted me, my past always there to remind me of the depths I had sunk to, standing in contrast to the professional I had become.

But other than myself, everyone else around me saw something else. They saw me as a leader, someone who would do well as a principal. Besides, all of my leads for jobs as a behavior specialist fell through, so their faith in me seemed valid.

Terry has been a wonderful husband and father, loving my children despite all the difficulties we initially faced. He was a stable father figure for them after their biological fathers remained estranged from them to varying degrees. Although the absence of their fathers hurt the children, Terry filled the void almost perfectly as they all developed a strong relationship with him. But it was more pronounced with my youngest child, who latched on to him as if she shared his genes. She adored him.

We seemed destined to be the perfect family I had always read about. It was not without regrets about the past and the approaching fears of the future, but it wasn't as threatening as it usually was because I had been to hell and back, as had he. Once you've made that trip, you always have its smell in your nostrils and the taste of it on your tongue. Although you never want to go back, you can still faintly hear the crackle of the flames in the distance.

Not being *enough* was the theme of my childhood and the remnants of that theme were still with me. Growing up, I never thought I was smart enough. As a teenager, I loved to play volleyball and had gotten good enough to be offered a scholarship, but I turned it down because I didn't believe I was good enough. My being held back in elementary school wasn't a particularly liberating thing also. I learned that one of the most prominent misconceptions people had was that education was for intelligent people and only smart people go to college. It was due to that experience I developed a voice for those who had a difficult start in life.

The scars I received left a mark on my psyche. I would have likely started college much sooner and would never have gotten into stripping if I'd had any confidence in my intellect. But instead, I slipped into survival mode, doing what I did to have enough money to stay afloat. Still, I am thankful for my past.

It has taught me that there is a place for everyone in education, if that is what they choose. Some people go to college; for others, it might be a trade school. It was also an option to matriculate at campuses or attend virtually, while some sail through it all with hardly a hiccup. Others need lots of support, tutoring, and interventions. But still, there is a place for them all.

I had received my high school diploma, which built my confidence to keep forging ahead. Then, when I went to college, I believed I could do just about anything, growing to trust my intellect each day. Just like that, I held that first degree in my hand. It was a fantastic moment that exploded my faith in myself, and I started referring to it as my first degree because I wanted to get another. I earned a certificate in biblical counseling, studying the Bible as part of my education. That sparked the desire to return to school to get a master's degree. Getting multiple degrees and certificates represented a major hustle for me, but with everyone's faith in me, I stared down another demon and chopped its head off.

The decision to get my doctorate was the biggest prize. It was the educational brass ring, and I was intent on seizing it. It was significantly more complex than anything I had ever done, but with so much success in my rearview mirror, I knew it was achievable. My difficult road to a doctorate taught me that anything worth having was worth fighting for. It may sound cliché, but it is more than just words that looked pretty on the page. It is the blood, sweat, and tears of my days and night, a fight comprised of sacrifices, studying early in the morning and late into the night. It was the fight of facing the committee to defend my dissertation. All of these represent the reality of genuine commitment.

Whenever we set out to do something of note, a combination of both great and small adversities will be thrown into our path. We often think that the difference between success and failure is intelligence, luck, or connections. But while all of that plays a part, the most significant part of anyone's achievement is their willingness to persevere, as perseverance can make up for what we lack in other areas. As a result of my troubled backstory and my desire to persevere, I've been led by a whole bunch of students who wouldn't hear a message of encouragement from someone born with a silver spoon. They believe me because they have visible proof that I did it too.

Of course, I wish my decisions could have been different, but there is a lot of beauty in my broken past. Never in a million years would I have thought I would have this fairy tale love, exceptional children, a rewarding career, and such a promising future. I didn't know anything could disturb this happy life we had made and was about to learn that was far from the truth. We would soon face a storm we had not prepared for and would have to find a way to weather through.

Many of my students today are fighting for education in a world where most kids simply give up. They do not fight for it, partly because they have to fight for their lives on a daily basis. Much of it is not coded, documented, or tracked, but it is visible all the time. Many of the families place a stronger emphasis on work than on education, which affects the disposition of the kid in that regard.

Additionally, they are facing challenges their parents and grandparents never did. Drugs have always been significant concern over the decades, but they are more accessible to students today than ever before. A student might be offered drugs several times a day, from their trip to school, during their several hours there, and on the way back home. In comparison, their parents, in their time, might have had to search for someone who had access to drugs. So, for parents, guiding their children past these landmines where drugs run amuck, and sex is a prevalent part of everything in reality. It's in music and on television, and an averagely intelligent kid can figure any of it out. I have to explain to them their worth constantly, and often, they break down crying. After all, they don't understand that they are worth something, because they feel a certain way about their involvement with drugs, teen parenting, gangbanging, or whatever else plagues them.

As Americans, we take so much for granted, causing us to climb up on our high horses as we bash others for wanting to leave their countries and come here. I have always been a firm believer in borders, as, without a border, you have no country. However, the notion of borders vanishes when I see these children in school and the teachers tasked with their learning. My heart breaks for these children, and I am compelled to teach, help, inspire, and cheer for their successes. They become my kids, sharing their joys and pains with me as they push for greater heights.

Unfortunately, the burden of taking care of these kids rests on the people who pay the taxes that pay the teachers, cover the costs of the infrastructure and feed them breakfast and lunch each day. This is even more of an issue if the school comprises a whopping amount of 90% of immigrants. Many hard-working people get up each day, working long, hard hours to pay taxes that cover these costs. The frustration of many on this issue is understandable, significantly when a school district is growing due to the influx of illegal immigrants.

Often, there is no room for these students. There are few chairs, desks, books, and square feet, too few to serve them. Yet these schools have to feed them for free and give them everything they need to get a solid education. Many immigrants indeed attend college without paying a dime, while American kids work multiple jobs or take out a year's-long loan to struggle to pay for their education. I see it all with a total understanding of both sides of the issue. I am reminded of doctors who have to treat criminals who get shot or terrorists who just blew up a building. Doctors don't refuse to treat someone because they disagree with their life choices, as they took an oath to heal all sick bodies. Teachers have a similar mission, duty-bound to teach anyone who sits under the sound of our voices, whether we agree with their politics or not. So, I can connect with the children's frustration in the school systems, particularly in Texas.

At the same time, black Americans are losing opportunities because they are not bilingual, thereby losing out to people willing to work for less because of their immigration status. All I can do is educate, changing the future of these students because I teach them to think and train them to learn. I remind them that they are valuable, no matter how they got here, admonishing them to take advantage of this golden opportunity by making the most of it. I talk to them about being productive citizens of society, and sometimes, my message penetrates their hearts.

It is true that our students have incredible struggles and seemingly insurmountable obstacles, but I also show them that the world is laid out in front of them. Along with their difficulties, they have a vast array of help available and thus shouldn't disappoint their families and their country by getting wasted on drugs. They have access to tutors, caring teachers, the internet, and a thousand programs designed to help them succeed, so there's really no excuse when the result turns out bad.

I wish someone had had that talk with me when I was still young and pliable, and before I doubted my abilities. Maybe then my choices in life would not have led to so many regrets. I regret that I wasted time getting into trouble, not realizing my worth. I regret that I did not pursue God's purpose for my life and did not have faith in the many talents that define me today.

But at the same time, I acknowledge regret as an utterly useless emotion, because we learn from our failures as much as we learn from our successes. The traumas I went through have become tools in the hands of God to help students see that they can come back from a very dark place, just as I have.

Perhaps it was my destiny to go through all those trials and tribulations. Maybe God knew I would make those bad choices. I believe that He gave me the heart of an educator, so that my adversities could be put to good use. Perhaps I had to suffer through it all so that I could help others. But now, I rejoice over His hands in my life, as things could have turned out much worse without Him. I could have been homeless or dead; from that perspective, there is no cause for regret. There is only thankfulness for the past, the present, and the future.

Today, I am working on re-releasing *Don't Date Him,* a book to help women make better dating choices. I also intend on returning to college in order to acquire another certificate as a counselor and my degree as a licensed chemical dependency counselor. Drugs are running rampant all over our state, and kids need someone who believes that they can get clean and sober, reclaiming their lives.

As for my biological children, I am proud of each of them. They had their bumps in the road, but just like all children, they had a decision to make, and they made the right one, pointing their lives in the right direction. I even have a wonderful grandchild to show for the struggle. Nicole has been a fantastic mother, reaching her breaking point and repenting before the Lord. As a result, the whole world opened up to her, and she started getting things together. She lives in a beautiful apartment and returned to school; her life filled with promise today.

Cameron had some tough days, hyperactive and dealing with his internal issues. At one point, I was deeply concerned when the school called to inform me that he was cutting himself as a coping mechanism. We had to kick into immediate action as a family and a school community to help him. But today, he is doing well and moving forward with life in positive ways. I am thankful for the power of prayer, as many of the kids he used to run with are now either in prison or strung out. So, every time I see him, I thank God he is doing well.

He decided that he would go into the military. Although afraid for him, I was so proud. Cameron wanted to serve his nation, which was noble and respectable. He started studying for the military entrance test, failing it the first time, but he persevered. Determination set in as Cameron studied daily, spending hours and hours in his books. In the process, he got into a car accident, damaging the car he was financing. He was devastated and thought it would hurt his record. But, when he finally passed the test and got enlisted in the navy, he let his creditors know that he would be leaving to serve his country. The finance company forgave him of that car debt because he was now in the military. It was like being given a new start in his life.

Children often have hiccups in life, and parents sometimes worry that their child's mistakes are fatal and unrecoverable. But instead, we have to trust God and our children to find their way just as we did when we were their age. All of Cameron's mistakes are in his past, as his life is nothing but great possibilities now. And that is the case for all my children. They get to seek God in their way, reaching for Him the way God reaches for them.

My youngest children, at the time of this writing, are still home with me and thriving well. They did not have the same struggles as the older two, so they didn't act out in the same ways. They got to learn much from their older siblings' experiences.

My journey from the strip clubs to the classroom was long and hard, a death-defying climb from a point lower than the bottom, to the top, with little more than perseverance to get me there. I love to bring encouragement and hope, informing them that I have danced to buy diapers and I know what it is to be in the pit of despair. I continue to speak when I am asked and train teachers in the school systems. But I will never give up my work to help emotionally disturbed students who have suffered trauma.

My daughter started making her beauty products, beginning with lipstick, lip gloss, and other simple products. She took the bull by the horns and started building her social media following despite being somewhat shy, doing dances on TikTok to make her audience. As a result, she created her confidence and is very comfortable talking to people now. She started raising a bit of money to help pay for her cheerleading expenses, which are constantly rising.

She wasn't making thousands of dollars, but the money she made was impressive. I continued to encourage her each time she wanted to give up, as I couldn't let her walk away from something that worked for her despite the prevalent challenges of running a business. I reminded her that there were people in their 30s and 40s who wanted to own businesses but could not figure out where or how to start. She was already ahead of the game and had to see it through.

I had lost a lot of my hair due to the stress and anxiety I was dealing with. So, together, we developed a hair oil to help restore my hair, and it worked. All the hair I had lost in the front of my head started to grow back, and the places where the hair was thin got thicker and fuller.

Before I started using the hair oil, I went to get my hair trimmer once a year. Now, my healthy hair grows so steadily that I have to go once every couple of months, and each of those times, my hair is longer and thicker. Everyone in the family was using the hair oil, with our hair shiny and beautiful. We knew we had to brand this product and get it out to the world, so we called it Hodge and Wilson hair oil. Although we didn't promote it as vigorously as it deserved, we were proud to have created it and kept it high on our list of priorities for the future.

In the meantime, the kids were busy with sports. For years, volleyball, basketball, and football were part of our family. They naturally got so involved and good at sports that they started to develop confrontational attitudes on the court and the field. If things weren't going well, they would argue with their team. I went to many games but couldn't stand seeing them angry with their teammates. It was too much for me to witness. But I had to learn to let them dominate the world they were living, working, and playing in without my interference.

For a long time, my name and face appeared in every newspaper in the Houston area, and I was being called around the country to speak at different events. My kids had spent a large part of their lives either dealing with bad choices or living in the shadow of their mother's publicity. But they were intelligent and diligent, and I never had to worry about their grades because they were independent learners. I had to be careful not to transfer the idea that they were not enough, that same idea that had plagued my own childhood. When I thought the idea of not being the best or good enough was starting to develop in my kids' minds, I let go and allowed them to work through the process as they have. And I am thrilled with how they progressively got better. My son is likely to be offered a basketball scholarship for college.

The most important aspect of their lives is their relationship with God, which has blossomed and grown through the good and bad. They all love the Lord. I have always kept them in church and depended on the Lord to remain paramount in their lives. They are open to praying to God even in tough times and have learned to trust Him to make things right.

In a final act of redemption, I wanted to clear my name in the justice system. Having that on my record affected my career because there were some places where I couldn't work with a misdemeanor. I collected as many signatures as possible and submitted them with my application for a pardon, including a copy of my doctorate and all my work in education. In 2019, the governor of Texas gave me a full pardon for my misdemeanor of public lewdness. My stain was removed, and my record was clean. It was the last act of perseverance I had to take. My past had come full circle, but my story is not complete. There is so much left to do. And now, now that I know I am enough, nothing is standing in my way. I know I am the woman to do it all by the grace of God.

EPILOGUE

All you have slowly perused thus far, probably having views and expectations of your own, amounts to my life's story. It has been a journey filled with a collection of bad decisions, but for reasons and methods you have already been made conversant with, things became different for me. I did not bring these things to your knowledge to be boastful or proud, but rather because of my desire to show God's incredible grace and power. I know that it is He who accomplished these things in me. Left to myself, I would have messed everything up, getting drained and then lost in the process.

Until now, there are moments where I catch myself immersed in the happenings in my life, overwhelmed at how things changed so rapidly, and undeservedly at that. Sometimes I wonder if my past makes me unworthy of God's blessings. Regardless of all the doubts that my mind conjures up, I depend on the Lord for everything and try to live my life as a reflection of his grace, serving only Him. No matter where you've been or where come from, Jesus' blood was shed for you, and the forgiveness that comes with it is yours for the taking. All you have to do is reach out and receive it.

We all have stories to tell, just like mine that you have just read. In this last chapter, I will be documenting lessons I have learned from my story. They can remind you to hold onto God's rope, even when doing so seems impossible.

Lessons on Family

FAMILY CREATES A JUNCTION WHERE YOU LEARN ABOUT UNCONDITIONAL LOVE and trust. If you have parents, or siblings who love you, provide a roof over your head and protect you from all that is bad and ugly, you should consider yourself one of the privileged few. I did not have a picture-perfect family and the absence of a biological father, coupled with my subsequent efforts to seek him out in others, later took a toll on me in ways I couldn't imagine. If you have a father concerned about your well-being, you don't know how fortunate you are. My former self would kill to trade places with you.

Although having a loving and supportive home is good for you, it is not an excuse to punish yourself if you don't. There are so many people in the world, including myself, who were not dealt with all the right cards in life but still managed to work things through. Even with no family in this world, you have God always looking out for you.

Lessons on trusting God and His plans

WE DON'T ALWAYS KNOW WHAT GOD IS UP TO WITH THE TECHNICALITIES OF our lives. It may seem obvious that we are headed for a brick wall, but we can never tell if it was in the cards from the beginning. Maybe that brick wall was designed to knock us back into reality, or better still serves as a barrier to keep us away from something decidedly worse. As we might never find out, we just have to trust God and His plans, as He knows us better than our families and closest friends. He even knows us better than we know ourselves.

In tough times, we learn that God's plan is better. Just like that student of mine so many years ago, we have to ask if we are up to following God or the devil. Although the devil has a plan for us just as God does, his goal is for our destruction, unlike God's, whose intent is for our good and His glory. We must, therefore, seize the plan of God even when it doesn't feel good or comfortable. Even when we don't understand, which tends to happen almost all the time, we can commit to following God's plan and believing that he will carry us through the wilderness into the promised land he designed for us.

Lessons on God, Faith, and Humanity

Events in my life demonstrate that if I am to trust anybody, it should be God alone. I have no idea where I would be or how my life would have turned out if I did not have faith in God. Every hardship has helped me realize that nobody in this world cares for you as much as God does. The only thing you have to do is to let Him decide things for you. As I mentioned before, as humans, we are 100% convinced that we know what is best for ourselves and the perfect means to face problems. But reality has a way of disagreeing. For instance, I used to think that the best way to improve my financial situation was to work at a strip club, using my body to attract paying customers. But it turned out I couldn't have been more wrong.

All the hardships I faced in my life brought me closer to God, and for that reason, I feel thankful that these problems found their way to me. They strengthened my faith in God and let me see my capability to overcome them. I understand that some people may not believe in God for personal and rational reasons. But I don't know what I'd have done without my faith and dependence on God. I doubt I would have managed if I didn't have God to turn to during those darkest moments. So having faith and making time to cultivate it is imperative.

Always remember your humanity. There will always be someone who could use a kind word or gesture. So, if you cannot find someone to be kind to you, be the source of kindness for others. You will always be compensated for it.

Lessons on Mistakes

I CANNOT STRESS ENOUGH THAT YOUR PAST DOES NOT DEFINE YOU. STILL, THAT doesn't mean you don't have to be careful with your present. Through my sojourn in life, I was used and abused in various ways, some of which were my fault. My engagement with the abuse of drugs and public lewdness followed me for what seemed like an eternity. Those were my mistakes, and they cost me heavily when I tried to embark on a career. Even though I eventually got past them, those mistakes made me realize just how important it is to make decisions carefully.

Remember the time I got raped? None of the other strippers responded to Jared's call except from myself, thinking it would just be an opportunity to make extra cash. How wrong I had been! My naivety and stupidity back then were precisely why those mistakes happened.

So, if you spend all your time beating yourself up about the bad decisions you make, don't be overwhelmed with the thought that you are too helpless to change things. Stop being the victim and take control of your life. For everything that happens to you, you can either run from it or stand your ground and face it.

God gave you a brain with sense, intelligence, and hundreds of beautiful abilities so they can be used. Learn from your mistakes, moving forward with your head held up high. There are bigger and better things awaiting you; all you need is faith in God and courage to help yourself get through it.

Lessons on failure and success

THERE IS LITTLE WE FEAR MORE THAN FAILURE, RUNNING WITH THE ASSUMPTION that they make us weak and cause us to appear incompetent. But that is not at all true. Our failures are master teachers doing a better job of guiding us than any lecture could. It is a real-time education about what works and what doesn't. When we embrace failure, not in the sense of giving up but in the importance of learning from them, extracting lessons that set us up for success becomes possible. In that way, failure becomes a friend.

Success, on the other hand, is always delightful. We love our victories and revel in our achievements, always wanting to share them with others and have them rejoice with us. But success can be just as scary as the notion of failure. They place expectations on us both from the world and ourselves, along with the responsibility that comes with it, as we may be called upon by society to be role models for others. Success also places us in another stratosphere, and our good enough level from before becomes no longer attractive to others and unacceptable to ourselves. The pressure of achieving more and striving to beat our last effort becomes enunciated, and it might feel as if the finish line is constantly being moved. As soon as we cross it, we see that the world has pushed the success line farther back and demands that we strive to reach it.

The great lesson of failure and success is like all the other lessons. Our reliance on God is the safest place to be in a world where we are judged each time we fail and push harder when we succeed. We cannot get caught up in the world's definitions of success or failure because it keeps floundering from one meaning to another. Chasing worldly standards will leave us frustrated and confused.

God's measure of success is simple. He says, "Follow me." It is the same message he spoke to his first followers and the message he speaks to us today. "Follow me!" When we follow God, it doesn't matter whether we fail or succeed by outward standards, as His strength is made perfect in our weakness. If we falter, He is there to catch us, forgive us, and place us back on the right road. If we succeed, He is there to guide us, give us wisdom, and show us where we should turn next.

Lessons on Love and Abuse

Most of my wrong turns were taken in the name of love, and the others, inclinations brought on by previous hurt and abuse. We all have our definitions of love and happiness. I used to think that if someone was physically present – if the other side of my bed wasn't empty – I was loved. It did not matter if the other person had hit me, lashed out at me, or made me feel less of a person. I saw it as love still.

I guess I confused abuse with love, which was one of my life's biggest tragedies. I thought that being treated like trash was just a part of being in a loving relationship.

It wasn't.

If you want to change somebody you claim to love, you don't love them that much. My revised definition of love is accepting people as they are rather than as you want them to be because anybody who truly loves you will never be wrong for your mental health. Every relationship comes with struggles, but one person cannot simultaneously be your pain and relief.

Lessons on Determination

MY LIFE ALSO TAUGHT ME THAT IF YOU WANT AMAZING THINGS TO HAPPEN, YOU have to be patient till you start seeing the fruit of your efforts. It might take a while, but it definitely will come. If you have a dream, protecting it must be your objective regardless of all unfortunate circumstances. Just wishing your life to change is not enough; you must work for it. If I had wanted, I could have remained a stripper, or let myself continue to believe that it was impossible to escape my drug addictions. But I am proud to say that I defeated that ugly sickness.

Even when I started substitute teaching and things finally started going my way, I was determined to go further. Resuming work only a couple of weeks after giving birth isn't an easy feat, and neither is leaving your children home while working crazy shifts, but I did it anyway. I did it because I was and still am determined to give my family a better life. For that, I would be willing to do anything.

Phoenix

I LIKE TO THINK OF MYSELF AS A PHOENIX, KNOWN FOR SACRIFICING ITSELF TO pain, suffering, and even death so that it could experience a rebirth of a stronger self.

It's like the Phoenix lets itself be broken down willingly only to build itself again from scratch, with a much stronger foundation than the last time. It is my spirit animal.

Like the Phoenix, I suffered, spending an insane amount of time crying over my fate and luck. Good things would happen to me but would be closely followed by a dozen terrible things. I have lost count of the times I have been heartbroken, but looking back, I can safely say that the darkest moments of my life led me to the brightest place.

Like the Phoenix, I rose from the ashes, from my destruction, and developed into a strong, independent woman with immense faith in God. Now, I am happy. Seeing my children around me equally happy also gives me further strength, just as devoting most of myself and my time to God and carrying out His word gives me peace of mind and heart.

Lesson on Contentment

I CAN FINALLY SAY THAT LIFE IS GOOD. YOU HAVE READ MY STORY FROM START to finish and can probably vouch that the road to a happy life has not been easy or scenic for me. But I will say that the journey is worth it – the relationship with God, the peace that comes from doing His work, and the satisfaction that comes from living as He intended.

If you are also going through a rough patch, remember that things will only improve if you try to change your circumstances. Human beings are limited in their abilities, but God isn't. So even when you are trying to change your circumstances, there is only a limited amount of heavy loading that you can do.

At some point, you will need God to back you up, as He is not limited in any sense of the word. His wisdom, love, and assistance know no bounds. All you have to do is to ask Him for help. No matter how often you feel you have disappointed God, find your way back to Him. There is one other thing that God provides in abundance: Forgiveness.

Forgiveness is multi-faceted. We must first ask God for His forgiveness as it frees us from the penalties of our wrongdoing. But we must also learn to forgive others. We free them from our wrath and condemnation when we forgive those who have wronged, hurt, disappointed, abandoned, exposed, and attempted to destroy us. But also, in forgiving others, we mimic God's love and compassion when he forgave us.

Lastly, we must forgive ourselves. This is the point where people can begin to see the difference in their daily walk. Failing to forgive yourself means walking around daily with the weight of the past following you like an anchor chained to your ankle, clouding your judgment and robbing you of opportunities, friendships, and love. We can't erase the past, and we shouldn't want to. History might have been good, bad, or ugly, but trust God to use it all. Every mistake, lie, and spin around the stripper's pole can be made beautiful in the hands of our loving Father, God.